CALL SIGN – 'ICEMAN'

An Alaskan Aviation Adventure

Wishing You Good Flights and Blue Skies Ahead !

Tony Priest

Tony Boyd Priest

AVAILABLE AS E-BOOK AND PRINT
AT AMAZON. COM - BOOKS

CALL SIGN – 'ICEMAN'

An Alaskan Aviation Adventure

Tony Boyd Priest

Second Publication:

Published in the United States of America

Published by:

ATC Publishing

P.O. Box 714

Sharpsburg, Georgia 30277

ISBN-13: 978-0692378496

ISBN-10: 0692378499

Although this is a non-fiction book, some elements cannot be verified as true and correct. Also some names have been changed and some are possibly incorrect.

"Experience is like altitude. The more you can draw on the more options you will have to get out of trouble when the time comes. That time will show up, sooner or later, in Alaska."   *Captain Tony Boyd Priest*

ACKNOWLEDGMENTS:

I need to acknowledge the hundreds of folks that I've been associated with in Alaska. From the day Jimmy said, "Hey Tone, you've got to get up here" to the day the Captain of our Alaska Airlines flight announced, after a perfect flight I must add, "Ladies and Gentlemen, welcome to Seattle. Thanks for flying with us today." My list is very long and includes aviators that have blazed the trails before all of us.

I am very thankful for:

My family, who lived the adventure with me and supported me in my work and endeavors in good times and in bad times,

People placed in my life as I believe that no one accomplishes anything of significance on their own,

My wonderful wife Judy for affording me the time to complete this work and

I am especially thankful for my Heavenly Father for his guidance, help and protection throughout my life.

TABLE OF CONTENTS

INTRODUCTION:

After being told a hundred times through the years, "Tony, you need to write a book!" I decided to sit down and share with everyone some adventures and misadventures that I and others have experienced in the Great Alaskan Wilderness.

While in the process of writing and recounting stories, it became apparent that the book would be a multi-faceted work and appeal to several groups of people. This of course includes aviation enthusiasts, but also adventurous-minded people from all walks of life who would like to take a good look into another world.

Some educational actual experiences are integrated into the book where as a pilot, you might pick up on some things to assist you in staying alive; as a passenger, you might gain some insight into what's in the mind of the guy up front.

Flying in Alaska is somewhat glamorous, exciting, challenging and inspirational. There are some days you feel you should be paying for a ticket instead of earning a living, but then there are some days you'll find yourself wondering what you're doing there, convinced you are not getting paid nearly enough!

It was while working for an Air Carrier in Las Vegas that my Alaska story begins. I was living my greatest adventure to that point, flying the mail in the Sierras between Las Vegas, Tonopah and Reno, Nevada. The Sierras are just as unforgiving as much of Alaska and it's pretty good training ground for someone wanting to go up to the North country. Where you have high terrain, weather, rocks and ice coming together, chances are, it's looking like Alaska.

During my two years flying those routes, I had spent most of my waking hours in Reno where I developed some great friendships.

Jimmy Gibson was one of those good buddies. He lived at Lake Tahoe and worked out of Reno for years. I had a great deal of respect for Jim, not only for his flying abilities, but also for the creative shenanigans he'd pulled here and there. Not only that, he was from my hometown, Atlanta, Georgia. Jim always had a twinkle in his eye and you could sense his adventurous spirit. He's the kind of guy that would make you belly laugh in a restaurant until you fell out of your seat.

Well, sometime during the spring in Reno, he pulled up stakes and headed north. I hadn't heard from him for a couple of months. Then one day, out of the clear blue, the phone rang. There he was.

"Tony, you've got to get up here! It's great! They've got Super Cubs, Cessna 206's, Barons, Twin Beeches and Queen Air's. You won't believe this, but the Super Cubs have tractor tires! Not really, they're called tundra tires like balloon tires for landing just about anywhere. Hey, they're looking for pilots. You're going to be rich with your background! Why don't you just pack your bags and drive on up?"

My reply was somewhat cautious I'm sure. Alaska - now that's a big step.

He talked about moose and bears and flying over the most beautiful terrain imaginable. On and on he went.

I did feel a little apprehensive about flying over the huge ice floes moving back and forth with the tide in the Cook Inlet.

He said, "Yeah, should you lose an engine and end up in the water, your T.U.C. is about two to three minutes from splashdown."

I later found out that the ice floes he described lay about 30 seconds after liftoff from Runway 24 at Merrill Field in Anchorage.

"Well, that sounds pretty interesting. By the way, what's T.U.C.?" I asked.

"Time of useful consciousness, but don't worry about that stuff. They'll teach you how to handle those kinds of things. Besides, hunting and fishing is great. Listen, I'm going to let George, the guy I work for, give you a call in a few days. Just think about it. It'll be the greatest adventure of your life!" he said confidently.

The next day the phone rang. "Hey, Tony, this is George Jones, 'without the guitar'. Are you going to come to work for us? We could really use you up here."

Two weeks later, my adventurous wife and I packed up our old Chevy to the ceiling, sat two wonderful kids in between all the boxes and hit the road, or should I say, it hit us? The Alcan Highway can be a long and rough road.

As the beautiful lights of Las Vegas slowly disappeared in our rear view mirror, our adventure began. We were on our way!

CHAPTER 1

THE ADVENTURE BEGINS

During our 12 day, 3,500 mile journey to Alaska, we took in some of the most beautiful scenery in the world. However, during the last half, somewhere along the Alcan Highway, we both vowed never to drive it again.

Our route took us up through Reno, Nevada where I said my good-byes to friends at the airport, my day apartment, the casinos, the good times and the bad times. From there we headed out on the most direct route to intercept the famous Alcan.

After traveling 2,000 miles, we felt we had made it more than half way and thought we were prepared for just about anything. Not so. As we launched onto the Alcan and began our 1,258 mile journey, our excitement rapidly turned to survival.

I imagine it was just about the worst road in the world. Even though it was June, we ran into areas of ice and snow in several mountainous areas. I had driven on a lot of rough roads, but none with rocks the size and shapes of these and something new, frost 'heaves'. Frost heaves are generally caused by the freezing and thawing of the ground in the permafrost areas. They tend to create continuous waves on the road, which forces you to keep your speed around 45 to 50 miles per hour. Anything above that, you begin risking 'bottoming out', literally destroying your muffler and exhaust system or worse. Due to this phenomenon, road construction and repair are going on continuously. Another not so wonderful memory was the large trucks and incredible dust on occasion.

The road typically consisted of approximately five miles of pavement, followed by five miles of dirt and rocks. Traveling on one of these unpaved areas, I had a low speed blowout (around 45 mph). After easing to a stop near the side of the road, I cautiously got out. We were in deep wilderness now and all of us were watching for bears or other varmints. I ended up struggling in the soft dirt trying to get my jack to work. Finally I succeeded, but then found the wheel was practically welded on. Eventually, after hammering and wrestling for about two hours, I managed to get the wheel off. I couldn't believe my eyes. A pie shaped rock was stuck in the face of the tire! I'd never seen anything like that before. Believe me; I was glad I had strapped two complete wheels to the top of our car in Las Vegas. I eventually used them both.

After getting back into the car, it felt great to be rolling again. We hadn't seen anyone during those two hours and were relieved to be back on the road.

We had only driven a mile or so when one of the kids said, "Dad, Bears!" Sure enough, a large Black Bear with two cubs was on the embankment, traveling the same direction as we were. As we rounded the curve, there was another car on the side. A family was wandering around the vehicle and the dad was fervently changing a tire. Been there - Just did that. I slowed to a stop and asked if they needed help. They didn't. I warned them about the bears coming their way just around the curve and offered to hang around. They insisted they would be fine so we continued on.

Planning fuel stops was another challenge during those days. At that time it was sometimes 300 miles between gas stations. With very little signage, more than once, we had driven past our planned stop for gas when, after 25 or 30 miles with nothing in sight, we had to double back.

One of the problems is that many times the lodges double as gas stations and might actually be located on a river or an airstrip off the main road. The side road to get there might appear as an old logging road simply going off into the wilderness. And, oh yeah, forget fast foods. Restaurants were few and far between. Many times during that trip, I used one of my old Vietnam tricks.

I wired a can of beans or stew onto the engine block, drove another 25 miles, then stopped for a good hot lunch or dinner. So, we began to learn some valuable lessons on the way, which actually began to prepare us for Alaska. First and foremost - Be prepared!

Some items that may save your day, in addition to a good tool box, are things like wire clothes hangers, heavy duty plastic bags, duct tape, gas cans, extra tires and wheels.

Next, beware of taking short cuts across the mountains in British Columbia. Regretfully, we actually did that. The climbing road continually worsened whereas we felt we were in danger a couple of times. Once after passing a work crew with puzzled looks on their faces, we found the rocky road getting much narrower. I would have turned around if I could have found a place in the road wide enough. I didn't. Backing down five miles of a curvy, rocky road with huge drop offs on both sides didn't look promising. We eventually made it to the top of some mountain and ended up in a remote Indian village.

Right about the time we entered the center of the village my muffler finally gave way. Yes, with villagers gathering around (we were about the only car in the village), I had to tear off the rest of the muffler, strap it on top of the car and try to proceed out of town in an inconspicuous manner. V8 Chevy, without a muffler, yeah right. No one seemed to speak English so I tried to be friendly and look tough at the same time as well as draw on my Cherokee ancestry and possibly look more Native American all at the same time.

If you've got some time I'd recommend the trip, at least once. In 1996 I drove from Denver to Anchorage again. It hadn't improved much. While there were more fuel stops, the road actually seemed to be worse.

I've heard some mixed reviews lately. On a positive note, one was that the road had been greatly improved with more stations along the way. It could be one person's perspective or maybe they're right. It's best to be prepared for the worst regardless.

Despite the road's condition it's got to be one of the most beautiful and pristine wilderness roads in the world. I plan to drive it again sometime in the future.

CHAPTER 2

OUR DESTINATION: ANCHORAGE, ALASKA

It was a cold, dark and rainy night when I and my family first arrived in the outskirts of Anchorage which I was later told was actually Eagle River, a suburb of Anchorage.

It was quite a relief to see the lights of civilization again after our long drive up.

As we entered town we found a rather rustic hotel showing a Vacancy sign and quickly pulled into the packed parking lot.

After I'd checked in, the clerk pointed to the stairs as the direction to get to our room. I glanced up to see the rooms were set up in an atrium style just like the old western movies.

I went out to the car and proceeded to get my weary family and baggage up the stairs and into our room.

Before going in, I glanced down at the main floor again which contained a large rather antique looking bar. In the center was a dance floor, surrounded by customer tables and various game tables.

Several dart boards adorned the walls. I wasn't really sure what that was about but there were several rowdy looking folks drinking lots of beer and playing the game.

We continued into the room and settled in for the night.

As the Alaskan night progressed, the noise from downstairs continued to get louder with an occasional fist fight that would jar us awake.

Several of the guys had been wearing guns earlier and a little after midnight, we were wondering what we'd gotten ourselves into. We both agreed that we had a distinct feeling of being somewhere back in time, living in an old western movie.

I guess no one was killed that night. Everything seemed perfectly normal the next day. The family was fine and seemed glad to stay in the hotel for the day.

I made a phone call to Jim and met up about an hour later.

We went into Anchorage and to his favorite restaurant. Once there he promptly began to harass the waitresses into submission. He seemed to be popular with them, always joking around in his deep southern drawl.

"Hey Honey, you got change for a dime?"

"Why the heck do you want change for a dime Jim?" she asked. "That's just plain stupid!"

"Well, Honey, I really wanted to leave you a tip today," he answered, all in fun.

During lunch, we talked about our days in Reno, college days in Atlanta, the Varsity restaurant, our trip up and he of course briefed me on what was to come.

"Well, Tone, you ready to meet George?"

"You bet I am! Thanks for lunch Jim!"

After a quick driving tour of Merrill Field, we went looking for George.

George Jones "without the guitar," was a tall swaggering Texan who was quite impressive to be around. There was no doubt he was the boss, the leader of a very large Alaskan bush flying company. His fleet consisted of aircraft of all types both fixed wing and helicopters. Everywhere I looked I saw strong individuals taking care of business. The guys were serious about their work yet relaxed. They were loading, unloading, cleaning, fueling and performing maintenance. Two guys, obviously pilots, were doing preflight checks on their aircraft for the next trip. I was reminded of a place and time not so long ago.

Many of his guys were hard core bush pilots who would and could go anywhere and do anything within reason. These guys knew a lot and I wanted to learn as much as possible from them.

I immediately liked George and was impressed by his operation. He quickly introduced me to some of his pilots. The Chief Pilot, Red Walker, was assigned to give me an introduction to Alaska flying and to see how I flew.

The next day I had planned to meet with Red for a training session, however, he ended up on a trip in the Twin Beech with no room for me to go. I was wandering around the ramp, observing all the activity, when George walked up.

"Tony, why don't you run over to Tyonek with me today? I'm gonna' take the 206 over, check out the runway and put a fish deal together."

"Sure...Sounds great." I replied enthusiastically.

'Isn't this a little sudden - Jumping out into the bush already? I can identify a Cessna 206, one out of three times. What's a fish deal? Where the heck is Tyonek? What kind of name is that anyway? What do you mean check out the runway? Do you mean land on it, to see if it's safe? Isn't that a native village? Do I need a passport? Do you have a life raft?'

CHAPTER 3

FIRST ALASKAN BUSH FLIGHT

As George motioned for me to follow him, "Yeah, Tony, we're planning to haul some salmon over for the Anchorage Cannery. Tyonek is only about 50 miles from here. We're using the Cessna 206 because it's the best equipment for today's mission. We can get in and out with a few hundred feet of decent runway. With 300 horses and the high wing, it's one of the best bush airplanes up here. Come on over to the office."

I followed George into the office. He stepped behind his desk, plopped down and leaned back in his wooden swivel chair. Leaning back, he turned, reached down and pulled open the lower file drawer. After shuffling a few papers for a moment, he lifted out a beautiful Colt .44 in a nice western holster. He kicked his chair back, strapped on the holster, pulled out the .44, spun the carriage and made sure it was loaded.

He looked up. "They ain't the friendliest bunch in the world." He opened the safe and pulled out a briefcase. "It's a cash deal."

Now, you've got to understand, I'm suddenly and definitely in culture shock. I later found out some of the Tyonek folks had been burned so to speak by not being paid for their fish on occasion. Now anyone coming along to 'take' their fish, even with cash in hand, was looked at with suspicion and possible hostility.

Although the village is close to Anchorage don't go there unless you've got business and you've been invited. We had a couple of airplanes come back with bullet holes in the wings. One had lost just about all the fuel in one wing and had a precarious landing back in Anchorage. A pilot with another company was shot dead on the runway after stepping out of his aircraft. Of course most folks in Tyonek were very friendly and helpful to us. Remember, this was more than 23 years ago. I'm sure a lot has changed through the years.

George, flying left seat, was professional and thorough on his checks before takeoff. He explained that Merrill Field was sandwiched between Lake Hood, the busiest seaplane base in the world and Elmendorf Air Force Base just to the north.

"I'd say it's best to really keep your eyes open around here," he said.

After being cleared for takeoff, we went roaring down the runway and were quickly airborne. The airplane climbed like 'a homesick angel.' That term I heard first in Alaska. I wondered why we were climbing so hard but in less than a minute I saw the reason why: Water, lots of it. I initially thought it was the ocean, but soon saw the other shoreline. The Cook Inlet is an arm of the Gulf of Alaska that is constantly fed by glacial waters from several major glaciers. These rivers of ice and water flow back and forth depending on the tides. After takeoff from Merrill Field or Anchorage International you're immediately over water, cold water, so the idea is to get to an altitude that will allow you to reach the shoreline should your engine let you down.

Some lesser horse-powered aircraft spend time following climb corridors to get to a safe crossing altitude. Believe me there are some horror stories of people not going by the golden rule of 'Always leaving yourself an out' and in this case not being within gliding distance of land. Splashing down a hundred feet short of the shoreline is likely a fatal crash.

At 2,000 feet we headed across the inlet and although the water was brown with silt, I immediately spotted some pure white whales swimming along near the surface. George called them Belugas and suggested they were feeding on salmon coming up the inlet.

As we approached the other shoreline, I spotted a couple of large bears feeding on what I assumed to be salmon. 'We took off five minutes ago and I'm already seeing bears!'

As we approached our destination George buzzed the village to let them know we were there. There wasn't much communication available in the villages in those days.

He then made a low and slow pass over the landing strip looking for anything that could cause a problem on landing or for taking off. I personally saw a lot of problems; narrow, dirt and gravel runway with mud holes, somewhat hidden by trees and trees on both ends. Take me back to Las Vegas!

George used all the right techniques it seemed as we landed smoothly, stopped and pulled into the turnaround area.

As we secured the aircraft, George said, "Tony, keep an eye on the plane. We need it to get home."

We locked the doors and began walking toward the group of native villagers that had come to meet us. As we converged, as a combat veteran, I immediately noticed several with rifles and side arms. They generally had dark complexions, were straight faced and dressed in jeans, colorful shirts and boots.

They were not threatening intentionally but just the presence of weapons put me on edge.

I thought possibly that this was probably a part of the negotiations. 'Don't mess with us' seemed to be their basic message. However, they became friendlier as we talked and I gradually began to relax with them.

With my own Native American heritage, I felt somewhat of a kindred spirit with them and sympathized with their plight in this clash of cultures. I found out later, they were carrying weapons for "bear protection."

George eventually got his deal made. They shook hands and as we headed back toward the airplane, "You ever flown a Queen Air or Beech 18?"

"No, to both, but I have quite a bit of Aztec, Seneca, Baron and Cessna 402 time," I replied.

"Close enough," he said as he rubbed his chin. "Alright, I'll get Red to check you out this week."

The short, soft gravel runway with trees on both ends made the takeoff as interesting as the landing. Throughout the experience, George gave me pointers on how to handle the short, rough airstrip and associated terrain and on how to stay alive out here.

Over the next few days, I trained with Red and finished my checkout in the Queen Air. The aircraft is a non-pressurized cabin class aircraft with stairs, powered by two Lycoming 340 HP engines with a 2,800 pound load capability. This one was stripped down, strictly cargo with two pilot seats. Usually there was no co-pilot, but occasionally, company personnel rode along to take care of business or maintenance.

Red flew with me for a few flights, showed me some techniques and expanded my thought processes concerning flying heavier equipment, utilizing short and soft field techniques.

It came out during our training, that last season; two pilots had crashed on takeoff just off the end of the Tyonek airstrip. Both were killed in the crash. Now that evoked a new realization for me. You lose an engine, single or heavy multi-engine, you will crash land in the water or on the beach, it doesn't matter. It's not good. You survive the crash in the water, you're freezing, hypothermic in less than five minutes. You survive the crash on the beach, you're covered with a ton of salmon and surrounded by hungry bears.

In that regard, I chose to fly in a safe, conservative manner and to become very good at taking off and at staying in the air. However, as I later found out –

"In Alaska, it doesn't always matter how good you are.
Sometimes, it's just the luck of the draw!"

As things turned out, I became very good at flying the Queen Air and found myself responsible for my first assignment - Tyonek!

CHAPTER 4

ASSIGNMENT - TYONEK

It was a general fact that you had much more help loading at the beginning of the day than at the end of the day. Summer days are very long in Alaska, depending on where you are and on sky conditions. Around the Anchorage area, it's still twilight around midnight and breaking day again around three in the morning.

On my initial run of the day to Tyonek, I generally had 25 guys helping to load, 12 to 15 on my second run and 3 or 4 on my last run of the evening. As it was daylight most of the time, I personally didn't know when to stop. I had to remind myself to quit before the next day. My standing joke was that I had to jump into bed, change days and get up. It seemed that way quite often.

One particular evening, we were waiting for the last truckload of fish from the beach to finish off my load. After a couple of hours and no truck, we decided to search for them. The runway area was quite a bit higher than the beach and was surrounded by trees. A small road had been built from the beach area up to the runway.

We checked with the guys on the boat and found that the truck had been loaded and left the beach over an hour ago. We then estimated they had possibly broken down. Tom, the foreman, said, "We better check it out," then ran toward the shed to get at the four-wheelers. The others followed.

As they were firing up the vehicles, Tom yelled, "Hey, better take this!" as he tossed a couple of rifles to the guys. They grabbed the rifles, checked to make sure they were loaded and spun off with dirt flying. The road was only three miles long, so where could they possibly be? What could have possibly happened?

Shortly, the sound of the four wheelers stopped. Silence… Then, I heard shooting and yelling coming up from below the cliff. Then silence again.

About 15 minutes later, the truck and four-wheelers came driving up to the airplane. The driver and passengers were grinning from ear to ear. The truck was covered with mud as was the salmon.

It seems that the truck had stalled momentarily on the muddy, wet road on the way up. Trying to restart, the driver, Robert, thought he'd flooded the engine. Their best option was to wait a few minutes before attempting another start simply because the battery was getting low. Suddenly, they felt the truck shift to the side.

Glancing back, they were surprised to see that a huge bear had just pounced on the back. Robert and the guy riding shotgun, swung their doors open simultaneously yelling and hoping to intimidate the bear. The bear merely glanced up for a moment and continued eating. Suddenly, two other very large bears broke through the bushes and bounded onto the roadway.

They both jumped back into the truck, slammed the door. Robert reached for his rifle. No rifle - Ambushed by bears and no rifle! What a predicament. After trying to start the truck a couple of more times, he realized the battery was practically dead and a start was not going to happen. Now there are three bears on the truck, grumbling at each other, having salmon for dinner. The main problem was that no one could get out of the truck to run the bears off.

They were very happy to see our guys on the four wheelers shouting and firing into the air. One thing they didn't need was a dead bear on the truck or in the road. Timing is everything in the fish business. A dead bear in either position could delay the fish haul for hours.

The bears got the message, moved away and ran back into the woods. The slightly shaken men finally got their truck running again and came on up the hill.

One of the guys looked at me and said, "Boy, I could sure use a drink!" I didn't blame him a bit. I wanted to get back to Anchorage and call it a day myself.

Luckily, they were able to pick through what was left of the fish and helped me get the last of the totes loaded. Sliding around on top of the plywood, I very carefully cinched down the load.

Finally, I said, "Thanks guys. Hope tomorrow's a better day! You know, the only ones today with a really bad day, are these salmon." They laughed; I closed the door and began crawling toward the cockpit.

I carefully ran the checklist, then woke up those 680 horses.

'No mistakes... It's late in the day... you're tired... runway's wet, mud holes, loose rocks, trees, bears, ice cold water. Bring yourself into focus!'

I started my back taxi toward the end of the soggy wet runway. After a rolling check of the engines and approaching the end of the runway, I eased off into the narrow turnout area. Without stopping, now looking over my left shoulder, I began bringing up the power on the right engine. My wheels were side-slipping in the deep gravel. By the time I was within 25 degrees of being lined up with the runway, I had full power coming up on both engines. The engines were really roaring now. I quickly checked engine instruments, ensured my fuel gauges had settled and began rapidly accelerating down the runway. Keeping the nose light in the gravel and engines roaring I eased back on the yoke. Suddenly four tons of aircraft lurched free of the gravel and began to move above the trees.

'Gear UP'. Now climbing 500 feet per minute, slowly, I began a very shallow left turn, crossed the beach and headed out to sea.

'Flaps UP... Going to cruise climb now - Don't need more than 3,000 feet.'

'Lots of blue water below me now...OK, 5,000 feet.'

'Was that a "Low Fuel" light I just saw flicker on my panel?' - Bears on shore, icy cold water under me. What had I gotten myself into?

The bright lights of Anchorage soon began to filter through the pastel twilight, seemingly dim at first, then getting brighter. I knew that soon I would be warm and dry again and be having a good meal with my family. 'Oops ...forgot! I've got to unload 2,000 pounds of salmon. Hope I have some help.'

Little did I know this was just the beginning of my diverse Alaskan adventure.

Although the fish haul season lasted only a few months, I had learned a lot flying the Queen-Air workhorse. We flew load after load off that short, rough strip and from other beach locations as well with no problems. A lot of credit goes to George, Red, Jim, Buck Rogers and some awesome maintenance guys like my friend Ben Jackson.   Ben was a pilot and mechanic who performed many miracle repairs for us. Red was "Red" because he had red hair I suppose. As Chief Pilot, he was one of the most experienced and the man to see about anything. "Buck Rogers, Pilot Extraordinaire," came as a handle for my good friend, Michael Lund. I'm not sure where he got that handle, but he was quite a pilot and worked alongside me with various companies through the years.

George was very successful that year and we all had made some money. However, if you plan to work hauling fish; be prepared for lots of long days, short nights and plenty of hard work. Although it was a good way to earn some great money you probably won't see me out there again anytime soon.

CHAPTER 5

TERMINATION DUST!

As summer and the end of fish season arrived, the whole atmosphere in Alaska began to change. The mornings became a little chillier; the smell of wood smoke drifted through the air and folks began dressing a little warmer.

Flocks of geese could be seen heading southward, although, I've often wondered about the geese leaders. Sometimes they appeared to be headed east, sometimes west and other times, even north! What's up with that? Being a pilot I tend to notice those types of things.

Shortly after the closest mountains are dusted, one of the major tasks at hand is to remove the float planes from the various lakes and streams throughout Alaska. Soon the wonderful lakes and streams begin to freeze. Lake Hood is a location where you can check the progress of the encroaching winter season. It's also interesting to see who doesn't get pulled out of the lake in time to beat the ice.

Many aircraft in Alaska are capable of interchanging the landing gear to wheels, skis, or floats, depending on the season.

Most, other than amphibian types, are sitting on floats only and have to be lifted out by crane, refit with wheels or skis, then either placed back on the ice when it's thick enough or parked in tie-downs or hangars. Some are simply winterized and stored until spring. It seems like there were always a few who didn't quite get the message and had to dig their float plane out of the ice. I guess that's pretty embarrassing and a difficult job.

As summer began to slow down, our pilot duties began to change. Shortly, many of the guys headed south with the geese. I discovered later that a lot of people did that and were given the name 'snow birds'.

The Alaska State Fair arrived and things were still very exciting to us as 'Sourdoughs' (First year Alaskans). I was at the fair one day when the skies cleared momentarily. A pilot friend of mine pointed and said, "Look, up on the peak - Termination Dust."

Now a term like that definitely needs some explanation. I responded, "What the heck is Termination Dust?"

"Aw, that's just the snow arriving on the mountain tops - Happens every year about this time. It's definitely the termination of summer. It won't go away 'til April or May," he said.

That little phrase, "Termination Dust," turned out to be a much dreaded phenomena with a lot of folks throughout Alaska. It represented the beginning of winter and bye, bye to sunshine.

Well, it wasn't long after, the Queen Air salmon trips tapered off and flight instruction was to become my main source of income. The following year was surprisingly full of wonderful experiences. I met a lot of Alaskans from all types of backgrounds who worked in various fields from oil to health care.

Many of my students were long time Alaskan bush pilots interested in upgrading their certificates and skills. These guys had amazing stories. At first I held my reserve, but later on, I learned firsthand there was truth behind their stories.

Being one of the most experienced flight instructors around, I was approached a lot by those guys in regard to instrument instruction. It was good diversity for me to fly and instruct in various exotic aircraft, a welcome break from Cessna 152's and 172's. By the way, if you're not a pilot, the Cessna single engine aircraft are used a lot in Alaska for one primary reason. Their wings are on top of the cabin and not below. Bushes and in the winter, snow berms are generally close to the edge of the runway and the high wings generally pass over the top. This is not always true, however. Occasionally, someone caught a wing anyway.

Anchorage and the surrounding Cook Inlet Basin provide a good training environment. Instrument training was great in that there were navigation facilities nearby and you were within a radar environment most of the time. Also, it's dark a lot during the winter, getting dark earlier on overcast days. However, even though you're close to Anchorage, you have to keep one eye on the weather at all times. It can change extremely fast, especially in the winter, when a 3,000 foot ceiling can suddenly drop to the ground right before your eyes.

Sometimes Instrument training is Actual Instrument training.
Where's the horizon?

CHAPTER 6

ARCTIC BASIN AIRWAYS

Arctic Basin Airways was a company and Flying Club I started out of necessity to keep working through the winter of 1983. My timing was good in so doing and over the next couple of years, with help from several enthusiastic club members, it became the premier flying and travel club in Alaska. My past experience and training as a Beech Aero Club Pro, in the early seventies, probably didn't hurt any either. We all learned a lot and had a lot of memorable experiences. I was privileged to have met and become friends with a lot of wonderful people.

Great pilots like Jerry Bagley, who just happened to be one of the best carpenters around and Ed Langdon, who was an FAA Designated Examiner were essential in putting things together. Aircraft owners that leased us their aircraft were just great folks in general.

Jay Harris and Billy Maxwell, who put in some cash to help us get started and other great pilots like Michael Lund, alias 'Buck Rogers,' and Mike Hopp, all helped put together an awesome force.

Of course, one of the primary reasons to take flight training is to attain the freedom to go places. In Alaska, it's generally more of a necessity than a luxury for most, as good roads are few and far between. Although I believe there's been some improvement, the general weather and terrain remain the same, which is very detrimental to road building and road improvement. Generally, 'you can't get there from here'.

Airplanes are a lifeline to anyone living 50 miles or more from Anchorage or Fairbanks.

It was somewhat of a novelty to actually use aircraft for flyaway trips like we did.

Durable Cessna aircraft
Arctic Basin Airways Flying Club

We visited places like Seward, a spectacular port city where we took a totally amazing Kenai Fjords Tour and some faraway places like Dawson City in the Yukon Territory.

Over the next few chapters, I'll attempt to hit some of the highlights of some memorable moments in time and begin with the wonderful trip to Dawson City, Yukon Territory.

CHAPTER 7

DAWSON CITY, YUKON TERRITORY

Our Dawson City Flyaway with Arctic Basin Airways turned out to be just about the best trip ever. We had five airplanes with every seat filled with excited people.

Our departure from Merrill Field in Anchorage was early in the morning. We were looking at a somewhat challenging several-hundred-mile jaunt through the remote Alaska wilderness. The weather was overcast, raining on and off, a typical summer day in Alaska.

All the pilots were thoroughly checked out and totally competent. We all knew we were in charge of the aircraft we were flying and ultimately responsible for our passengers' safety.

Operationally we kept visual contact on the aircraft in front of us throughout our journey. We also kept communications working on the air-to- air frequencies. This worked well for us navigationally as well and helped ensure all could observe optimum points of interest.

As can often happen in Alaska, within an hour of takeoff, the ceiling began to drop. Knowing we would soon be getting close to the twisting, spectacular canyons around Sheep Mountain and with lowering visibility, I made the call for everyone to return to Palmer (PAAQ). The plan was to wait out the weather and if no improvement, call off the flight. You could feel the disappointment in the air even though no one complained.

Everyone landed safely in Palmer and the wait was on. Not much to do in Palmer at that time, but they did have a small, heated building where we could keep warm.

There were a couple of decks of cards and we soon got a game going. Although it felt good to be safely on the ground and out of the rain, it wasn't exactly the type of day we'd set out for. Suddenly the door burst open. Buck charged in the door,

"Hey Tone. Breakin' up... Looks a little better out to the east. Mind if I head out and take a look?"

I threw on my jacket and followed Buck outside to find the weather indeed seemed to be moving on. I'd recently checked Gulkana and Northway weather which were both good. These two towns were on the other side of the pass and along our route of flight.

"Actually, that sounds great Buck. Matter of fact, why don't you take about a 10 minute lead, then we'll all take off. Are you up for blazing the trail for the rest of us?" I asked.

"OOOHHHHHH Boy!" This was Buck's favorite saying. "Let's do it!" he said enthusiastically.

After a quick walk around, he fired up the engine and taxied to the runway. We watched him launch and turn toward the pass. The roar of his engine soon became a drone as he turned and disappeared behind the first mountain of the pass.

The view from here was a little intimidating to some.

"Everybody in?" I asked. Making sure everyone was game for this adventure.

"You bet. Let's get going!" Half were already getting in their aircraft and belting in.

As the leader of the group, I checked that all had their engines started. Like the Blue Angels we taxied out in formation toward the end of the runway. Pretty soon our small fleet was airborne and headed in Buck's direction. We were taking our time entering into the unknown conditions of the pass, hoping to get a report from him.

Shortly, we heard, "Ladies and Gentlemen, this is Buck Rogers, Pilot Extraordinaire, reporting the pass at Sheep Mountain is clear. I am proceeding on to Gulkana. See you there."

"Thanks a lot, Buck. We all appreciate your help."

What absolutely gorgeous scenery! Total wilderness and, yes there are tons of sheep on Sheep Mountain. It's awesome to be looking at them at several thousand feet, standing on their precariously small rock ledges. I'm sure we were quite a sight for them as well as we flew by in a line.

Shortly after passing over the awesome Matanuska Glacier, we broke out of the clouds completely and were greeted with awesome blue skies.

Then, off to our right, appeared the white, snowcapped mountains marking the beginning of the Wrangell Mountain Range. Everyone scrambled to find their sunglasses as we passed the snow covered peak Mt. Baker. At 13,000 feet, it's the tallest mountain in the Chugach Range.

The entire trip was filled with awesome scenery and wildlife.

We thoroughly enjoyed our time in the sun, taking tons of pictures of our beautiful pristine scenes.

After our fuel and rest stop in Gulkana, we again launched, in trail of our path finder, Buck and were on our way to Dawson City, Yukon Territory!

After a nice flight through the Mentasta Pass, we were clear of most of the mountainous terrain. Thinking we had clear running now, everyone began to get excited about our destination.

However, as we approached within 45 miles of our destination, the weather again began to deteriorate. And again, everyone started to get the sinking feeling that Dawson City may not happen. We really didn't have a safety problem as we had fuel reserves to get back to the good weather at Northway, Alaska. However, as we drew closer to the ominous gray mass looming ahead, the airways grew very quiet.

I eased the P.T.T. switch down, "Hey Buck... you out there?"

The silence was screaming at us at this point - 'Time to make a decision'. All we could see was a mountain of gray clouds hanging over the Yukon River valley. I asked everyone to slow down to 80 knots and unless we heard from Buck, we were headed back to Northway.

Suddenly, the silence was broken, "OOOOOHHHHH, Boy! Hey Tone."

"Go ahead Buck," I answered.

"I'm looking at a city in the bend of the river. Bunch of old paddle wheelers stuck in the mud. Man, this river's awesome! You guys need to fly south for about nine or ten miles, watch for an opening to the east, ease up over the ridge and drop down on the river. Ceiling's about 1,500 feet. You're gonna' love it. See you on the ground." Buck said cheerfully.

Aerial view of Dawson City, YT. - "Where's the Runway?"

Now, I've got to tell you, that was music to everyone's ears. We all followed Buck's lead, travelled 10 miles south and low and behold, a nice wide opening in the fog and clouds appeared, just as our path finder said. We flew up and over the ridge, then dropped down on the river. Perfect! What a guy!

That was one huge river. It looked a lot like the Mississippi, except there's more of a river valley surrounded by mountainous terrain.

The shoreline was littered with old ship wrecks. As I rounded a bend in the river, 'Whoops, that's a live steaming paddle wheeler, better get a little higher'. Easing the 172 Sky

Hawk up 500 feet and a little to the left, we got a bird's eye view of a working paddle wheeler in action.

After a couple of victory turns over the city, we all landed safely on the hard-packed gravel runway. As the Custom Agent approached us, we realized, 'oh yeah, we're in another country'. Canadian Customs Agents were great and seemed glad to see us. We were done quickly and went about securing our aircraft for the night. As our group left the ramp, someone let out a cheer, "Yeah, Buck!" After a bunch of high-fives and cheers for Buck Rogers and each other, we headed for our hotel. Success!

S.S. Keno, a Paddle Wheeler from the early 1900's being restored.

Fate of many paddle wheelers who lost their battle with the
mighty Yukon River.

Yukon Territory, Jack London, "Call of the Wild" – sound familiar? Jack London lived south of Dawson City prior to the gold rush of 1898. Robert Service, famous author of 'The Cremation of Sam McGee' and 'The Trail of Ninety-Eight', lived in Dawson City until 1912.

There's lots of information and memorabilia on both authors located here.

Robert Service cabin preserved exactly as he left it.

What an awesome feeling it was, to stand in the doorway of Robert Service's cabin and see his lantern-lit writing table, note papers and books. He worked in quite a different environment than the comfortable work spaces we have today. With 40 below temperatures on the dark, long Yukon winters, living must have been generally tough. Both writers had to be a very hardy sort themselves. Even under those extreme conditions, they both managed to write some great works. Can you imagine the day to day life they must have experienced? Standing there, taking it all in, we realized we had taken a trip back in time.

Inside the Robert Service Cabin

As we left the old cabin, we headed down Main Street. The streets were dirt with some gravel and bordered by wooden boardwalks. Many of the old buildings had been preserved and restored to their original condition. The old buildings, the wooden boardwalks and the dirt streets filled us with the feeling of the old west. That is, right up to when a couple of large huskies came walking by. I started looking for 'Sergeant Preston of the Yukon' right away. That happened to be one of my favorite shows in the early years.

As we wandered through town, checking out some of the local folks, I remember commenting, "You know, it's amazing that everyone's dressing the part."

Then we came up on Diamond Tooth Gertie's Saloon.

We climbed up the old stairs and entered the foyer. There was a large hand written sign and in bold letters;

CHECK GUNS AND KNIVES HERE

"Wow, just like the Old West!" someone commented.

Later we found out that was not a joke. You checked your guns and knives at the door! Glancing toward the back of the coat room, I saw possibly a hundred weapons of all sorts; shotguns, rifles, pistols and knives.

As I was standing there mesmerized, one of the saloon gals patted me on the shoulder, "That's a nice leather jacket. Would you like to keep it?"

"Yeah," I replied.

"Then you better give it to me for safe keeping," the woman said seriously.

As we soon found out, this was a real saloon with real cowboys and Indians. Actually, it was a crossroads for all types of people from all over the Yukon, including hunters, trappers, gold miners and just about every other rugged type of profession there is. We all felt like aliens dropped into somewhere in the past. Saloon girls, drinking, gambling...the guys thought it was great. When the Can-Can dancers started up, we all scrambled for chairs only to discover our ladies suddenly needed to do some shopping.

Needless to say, they were not leaving us unsupervised at Diamond Tooth Gertie's Gambling Hall, "The northernmost casino in the world." Soon we were back on Main Street and began exploring the rest of the town taking in lots of culture and history.

"Anyone seen Buck?" one of the ladies asked.

"Wonder if he's still at Gertie's?" someone else asked.

"I believe he's at the museum," I responded.

Later, we heard there was a salmon bake down on the river that night. We arrived at the dock and soon found you had to take a small riverboat, the Yukon Lou, to an island up river for the dinner. As we boarded the ship, someone commented, "Hey look at the Captain. He really looks the part."

I glanced at the gruff old seaman standing behind the Helm. His face was weathered with a full beard. His gray hair exploded out from his worn but white ship captain's hat. He wore an oversized Navy pea coat, dark blue pants and heavy boots.

We weren't sure if he was smiling or not but from the squint in his eyes, he seemed to be.

"Looks the part? He *is* the part!" I said.

Later on, while underway, we did get to visit with him and got to hear a couple of great River Boat tales.

Evidently he was an experienced river boat captain in that he did a great job negotiating the radical currents of the river. Along the way, he pointed out several shipwrecks strewn along the banks. What an awesome sight.

Can you imagine how much life was lived, how many stories remain untold, the emotion, the excitement, the horror of having such a disaster on your watch?

There are many in Dawson City I'm sure that can fill you in on the history of the place, including stories of these shipwrecks, possibly through eyewitness reports.

After an hour or so on the paddle wheeler, we arrived at our destination. He carefully nosed the boat up to the shore of a heavily treed island.

The crew threw out the anchors and lowered the three foot wide gangway onto the river bank. Adventure anyone?

Very carefully, we all walked the plank, so to speak, onto this remote island in the middle of the Yukon River. No one knew exactly what to expect. However, we were pleasantly surprised and relieved to see a very large, rustic kitchen, all outdoors of course, along with tables enough for our large group. The meal, a wonderful outdoor salmon bake, was filling and unbelievably delicious.

Afterwards, we had another hour or so to explore more of the island. We discovered remnants of shipwrecks, various pieces of heavy equipment and other signs of previous inhabitants.

Native American Fish Wheel used for catching salmon.

The trip back down river was a little faster than our trip up of course and it felt good to be in sight of the city once again. As we departed the ship, we all thanked the captain of the Yukon Lou for a safe and wonderful journey.

After a couple of great days exploring Dawson City and the surrounding area, we began our journey home. The weather was good. Buck led the way.

Everyone had a lot of fun actually using our aircraft to go somewhere as unique and exciting as Dawson City, Yukon Territory. We had learned a little about the Klondike and had an awesome, incredible experience.

Wonderful lifetime memories were created.

Tony and Jerry at Gertie's Saloon.

CHAPTER 8

KENAI FJORDS

This wonderful trip happened the following summer and created more lifetime memories for some of our club members. Seward, Alaska was the destination after exploring the magnificent passes to Seward and then taking in the Kenai Fjords boat tour.

A somewhat shorter flight than the Dawson City fly-away, the Kenai Fjords trip was absolutely great. The route took us south, across the Turn-again Arm, over Hope, where we entered Resurrection Pass.

Southbound now, we passed over the lower and upper Russian lakes, then followed the Resurrection River to Exit Glacier. At that point just around the bend to the right, Seward came into full view.

The city was almost totally surrounded by majestic snow covered mountains reflecting in the sea green waters of Resurrection Bay.

After all landed safely, we headed for the docks. At the time, the Kenai Fjords boat tour was run by some wonderful friends of mine who gave us a great deal for the day. Could you imagine how we felt, having flown through pristine mountain valleys, landing at an unbelievably beautiful airport setting and then boarding a beautiful 50 foot touring boat for an all-day, spectacular sea-life tour? We even had a hot lunch sitting in front of a calving glacier.

One of the many glaciers you will see on a Kenai Fjords tour.

Natural Architecture - Unequaled Beauty

These rock islands are generally filled with birds and other wildlife.

The captain was highly skilled and knew the area intimately. From Puffins to Killer Whales, she knew where they were to be found. I highly recommend this trip for everyone. If you're not up to flying, there's also a good road and a railroad that will get you there. Regardless of the way you get over there it's all beautifully spectacular.

A remote and pristine wilderness, accessible by boat or float plane.

These boat tours are totally awesome for anyone who wants to see wild Alaska up close. The captain and crews were very helpful and took great care of everyone. The lunch we had while quietly drifting next to the glacier was unforgettable.

ABA club members returning from the wild and beautiful Kenai Fjords. Club member Virginia Vale is taking the picture.

Our journey home was equally scenic and enjoyable. The primary goal, as always, was to have an educational, safe and incident free fly-away adventure.

CHAPTER 9

FUN AT THE AIRSHOW

During the time at Arctic Basin Airways, I worked hard at developing my skills as well as my student's skills. Delving deep into aircraft performance charts and practicing flying at the edge of the envelopes, I managed to create some maneuvers of my own. I basically learned how to get the most out of the machines. The maneuvers, "Blind Canyon Turnaround" and "Short Field Bush Takeoff" were not found in books, but when flown correctly by a skilled pilot you can get the ultimate performance of the aircraft. Details of those and other maneuvers will appear in 'Call Sign – Iceman II, A Survivors Guide to Flying in Alaska.'

The 'Short Field Bush Takeoff" paid off in a fun way on a sunny, unusually warm 70 degree day at the Birchwood Airport Air Show. Birchwood, located just north of the anchorage area was normally a quiet airport. With its' paved strip, it was a popular place to do touch and goes with our students. It sits at the edge of the famous Knik River and is basically on the edge of the wilderness of Alaska. The elevation is close to sea level.

ABA Flying Club's Cessna 172XP at the air show

I had my son Paul aboard our Cessna 172XP and landed at Birchwood with little over half tanks of fuel. We parked the airplane in general parking and were having a great time wandering around, looking at airplanes and watching aerobatics, when the MC announced, "30 minutes left to sign up for the short field takeoff and landing contest."

After a little contemplation Paul and I strolled over to sign up. As we approached the podium, the MC asked, "Good morning. Is this your bombardier?" as he looked down at Paul.

"This is my son Paul. He's flying co-pilot today."

"Alright," the MC said. He turned and spoke over his shoulder.

"Hey Bill. ...Any age restriction on bombardiers?"

"No. Where's he at?" He chuckled as he leaned over to say hello to him.

"Well, here are the rules. You do a short field takeoff, from the line over there." as he pointed at the line near the end of the runway.

"Then, you fly around the pattern and drop three flour bombs on the target area over there." He pointed vaguely off to the side of the runway. "Then, you come back around and land on or beyond the line and stop as short as possible. All the measurements will be taken by the judges standing by."

He handed me the three flour bombs, which were basically about one-half pound cloth sacks of flour. I turned around and handed them to Paul, "Here you go son. You're my official bombardier."

"I can't be a bombardier Dad. I don't know what to do."

"Don't worry. It's simple. I'll watch for the target and when I tell you, open the window and throw them out.

"OK, if you're sure," he said.

"I'm sure," I replied.

The takeoff was great. No one watching could believe that a stock Skyhawk XP could be airborne in 220 feet. According to the judges, we actually were off at 190 feet but one of my tires had touched at the 220 foot mark.

That was all pretty exciting and as we began our turn downwind.

"Get ready, Paul," I cautioned.

"Ok." He gathered up the flour bombs to the ready position.

"Ok, open the window," I said. Paul nervously opened the window. The wind rushed in making it extremely noisy.

"Ten seconds to the target," I yelled. The seconds ticked away as the target disappeared under the nose of the aircraft.

"Three... Two... One... Ok.... Bombs away, I yelled." Paul just looked at me.

"Bombs away, Paul!" I yelled a little louder.

"What's bombs away mean?" he asked.

"Throw them out the window!" I yelled.

"What?" he asked again.

"Throw the bombs out the window!" I yelled in a somewhat frustrated tone.

He turned and threw them out, one at a time. As he closed the window I said, "Good job Paul! Now, let's see how short we can land this bird."

It's a good thing it was all in fun. Our training program had consisted of a short discussion on the way to the airplane. Plus, the use of different terminology over the target didn't help matters any. I heard we had people running for their lives.

The landing was fairly short; however, I caught a wind gust in the flare and floated a little.

As we taxied in to parking, Paul spoke up sounding disappointed. "Sorry dad, I think we missed the target."

"Not to worry about that son. You did great!"

How many 10 year-olds would open an airplane window in flight? He was a winner as far as I was concerned.

The results put us in second place for the short field takeoff and fourth place for the short field landing. Now, considering we had our beautiful red and white, stock Cessna 172XP up against stripped down Cessna 180's and 185's, that wasn't too bad.

After watching the awards presentation for a brief time, we headed off to look at a couple of interesting vintage aircraft. We were suddenly interrupted by hearing our names blaring from the speakers overhead, "Tony Priest and Paul Priest please report to the podium for a special award." What could this possibly be about?

As we stepped up to the podium, "Tony and Paul Priest, we of the Alaska Air Show Association would like to present you two with our most prestigious award." As he handed the trophy to us, he said, "You two managed to miss the bombing target farther than anyone in the history of our air show!"

Everyone got a good laugh. The trophy was interestingly cute I guess. It was on a stand, made of wood, with a large screw going through it. I guess that meant we had really screwed up.

I wouldn't trade the experience with my son for a million dollars. I don't know how much character it built, but it gave him a good story to tell at school. I also found him to be quite a courageous kid that could be cool under pressure. He's like that today.

The short field technique I developed for this performance proved to be very valuable in the coming years of bush flying in Alaska.

I can't take full credit for this feat however; it took some incredible engineering by Cessna Aircraft Corporation to build a stock aircraft with this capability. 200 foot ground roll... who ever heard of it? There's no wonder Cessna has the most popular aircraft in Alaska.

CHAPTER 10

ICE SAILING ANYONE?

One Saturday morning I was sitting in the Arctic Basin Airways clubhouse, feeling warm and comfortable, gazing out our large, picture windows. This was a rare treat for me, as normally I'm out in the elements doing something. Sipping on a cup of hot cider, the scene I was enjoying was an incredible Alaskan winter gale ripping across the airport.

There was no aircraft movement at the airport. The only movement was the blowing snow. The only sounds were the flapping of the wing covers on our aircraft.

Suddenly, I heard, "Hey, Tony lets go flying!"

As the words rang out across the room, I knew it was Steve Shaw, one of my progressing instrument students. Steve was a great student who owned one of the most beautiful Cessna 180's I'd ever seen. The 180 Cessna is a 200 horsepower, four seat tail-dragger. Tail-dragger is slang for an aircraft with a tail wheel instead of a nose wheel. This one was immaculate, well-equipped and had new paint and interior.

Now, I had done my best to teach these guys the rules about flying professionally and given the current weather conditions, you could understand my shocked look at the mere suggestion of going outside, much less flying. The weather was overcast and about 25 degrees. The runway was pure glare ice. The winds were, at least to me, a significant and serious problem.

"Steve, didn't you look outside?" I asked. "The winds are blowing 45 with gusts of 55 straight across the runway! It's a direct crosswind and the crosswind runway is not available due to construction, not a pretty picture! All our aircraft are grounded. All training flights have been canceled for the day. The airport is like a ghost town!"

"Oh, come on! I've got to head back to the village tomorrow. It's perfectly safe. I wouldn't think of bending my airplane. There's no crosswind strip at the village. I take off in this stuff all the time," he retorted.

Now, I knew Steve was a great pilot and had a ton of bush experience, plus he had worked and lived in a remote village for several years. I contemplated my several thousand hours' experience where I'd flown all over the country and I'd never heard of anyone taking off in a tail-dragger in 50 mph crosswinds particularly on glare ice. However, he was very convincing in his argument that he did this all the time at his village and he wouldn't do it if it was unsafe.

It was a tough decision, but I figured if he was so convinced he could take off and land I could give him some 50 knot crosswind holding patterns. I figured no one in their right mind would be in the practice area and we might even accomplish something.

We bundled up and struggled out to the airplane, which was being held down with 200 pound concrete tie-down anchors. (Drilling holes for anchor tie-downs is very tricky in Alaska, plus they are hard to find under the ice and snow.) He untied the tail and pulled the front chocks before untying the wings. Just sitting in the airplane felt like we were already flying. This airplane will take off at 50 knots. After a smooth start, Steve powered up and called ground control, "Ready to taxi."

"Who?... What do you want to do?" the tower replied.

"We want to taxi to runway six for takeoff," Steve matter-of-factly responded.

"Roger that... Cleared to taxi to runway six." The controller then added, "The winds are 330 at 47 peak gust 58." This meant that the winds were from 330 degrees and perpendicular to the runway direction and our takeoff path of 060 degrees.

Now, I saw four controllers standing in the windows of the control tower, probably taking bets as to whether we'd make it or not. I'm sure as we began to taxi that our audience continued to grow.

Steve's technique was to literally wind sail the aircraft over the ice while keeping the nose in varying angles into the wind. As he began slipping diagonally across the ice covered ramp, I finally got the idea. He simply kept crabbing into the wind with his oversize tires slipping easily on the ice. The ice was so smooth and deep, there was no chance of the tires grabbing on the asphalt.

After being cleared for takeoff, Steve eased the throttle forward and pulled onto the runway - facing north! The engine accelerated smoothly as he added a small amount of downwind rudder, just enough to begin to track along the center of the runway. The tail came up and away we went, practically flying sideways along the runway. With a four to five second ground roll, I never noticed if the tires had turned at all.

After clearing all the obstacles, getting out of the gusts and into smoother air and of course, catching my breath, I burst out, "OK! Alright! Nice job, Steve. Learn something new every day! Let's head on out to Big Lake and do some work. Let's see if you can stay within 10 miles of the VOR in a holding pattern. Plan to hold on the 270 degree radial and what type of entry do you plan to use?"

Steve did a good job considering the winds were 50 or 60 knots at the VOR. (VOR means Very High Frequency Omni Directional Range, a Navigational Aid placed in optimal areas for navigational purposes of aircraft.)

Believe me, as time went on, I found both situations, the ice and the wind on the runway and the wind in the holding patterns to be extremely valuable later on. I've always learned something from my students. This was especially true in Alaska.

After holding for some time, I figured he'd had enough. I didn't know why the beads of sweat were dripping from under the hood. A hood is a device to block the pilot's view of the outside, limiting his view to the instruments in front of him. For those of you that have held in 50 knot winds, you know why, especially if your instructor makes you do multiple entries and hold perpendicular to the wind.

We finally called approach and asked for clearance to Anchorage International and requested an ILS with a low approach to minimums and break-off to Merrill Field. The ILS is short for an Instrument Landing System precision approach. Generally it can take you down to within 50 feet of the runway.

The controller's attitude was like, "Sure... Do anything you want...You're the only aircraft in the sky." Steve was glad to be headed home, but I wasn't sure. I was thinking ahead to an icy runway landing coming up.

He nailed the localizer and executed a beautiful ILS to a 200 foot minimum, did our low approach and headed to Merrill Field. He elected to land on the same runway as the winds were pretty much identical. His technique was the same ice-wind sailing technique and it worked smoothly. There was very little ground roll (or should I say ice slide). We ice-sailed down the runway a short distance, exited the runway, did a reverse turn, slid a little tail first and proceeded down the taxiway. After sailing into the ramp area, Steve parked into the wind over the tie-downs. I got out and chocked the wheels as he shut the engine down. He pulled out some two by fours with rubber straps attached and placed them over the top of the wing. He explained that they acted as spoilers for his wings. This meant that if the winds got worse, his airplane wouldn't go flying across the ramp.

The winds did worsen through the night. The next morning following the storm, we discovered a larger and heavier Cessna 206 on its back. Everyone was sick to see the sight. We were lucky that none of ours was damaged.

Everyone was sick to see this beautiful Cessna the morning after the storm.

If you're thinking about flying in Alaska, be aware that many survival techniques and skills are not taught in the Lower 48 and are not included in text books. I believe on that day, my awareness of the capabilities of the aircraft we fly and of the skilled pilots who fly these machines in Alaska, was greatly enhanced. I must warn you however that I don't know of very many places with windblown glare ice deep enough or smooth enough to safely and confidently ice sail on a runway with a wheel airplane. The danger as we all know is catching a piece of asphalt and breaking a wheel or worse.

CHAPTER 11

A WORD TO FUTURE ALASKA PILOTS

The previous chapter brings to mind a point I would like to make regarding those of you who desire to fly in Alaska for a season or for a few years:

"Alaska is not a good place to build time for low time inexperienced pilots."

And old adage states... 'Experience is the best teacher', however, when it comes to aviation in Alaska, this is not necessarily true. Other pilot's experiences are extremely valuable, especially if you're teachable and wise. If you're determined to make the journey, read everything you can on the subject and try to find a good mentor who has been around a while. It's better to have flown a few hundred hours before even considering going north. The basic stick and rudder flying has to be natural. It's as simple as this. A small mistake or poor judgment call in Kansas might work out ok, but the same mistake in Alaska may be your last. Also, it's a good idea to flight instruct in Anchorage or Fairbanks for a year or so to learn from those long time bush pilots. Learn how they managed to stay alive out there. Then your chances for longer term survival begin to improve. Always be open to learning something from others especially when you're new in their world.

"Some pilots seem to have more guts than technique. Becoming a successful pilot in Alaska is a learned trait that takes time and experience. Learn and master the skills and get to know your own personal limitations."

Plan to take FAA Safety and Survival courses. Know the aircraft you're flying (or flying in) and always be prepared with emergency gear, even on short flights.

Always file company or FAA flight plans and most of all, as Clint, says, "Man's gotta' know his limitations."

During my time with ABA as a flight instructor, I firmly believed I had learned as much from my students as I had taught. Floats, tundra tires and skis were just a part of the diversity in equipment. As far as diversity of the people, well, you've got to be of a different sort just to live in Alaska!

To fly in this vast, wild country, I believe it takes a certain type of person. I found most of my students and pilot friends through the years to be very mission oriented. In other words they were determined to accomplish whatever goal they were assigned or had given themselves.

Not all our students and pilots were macho male types either. We had several females that demonstrated the perseverance it takes to become a pilot in Alaska. Several wonderful ladies such as Bev Holding, Wendy Agen, Susan Metcalf, Dianne Tarrant and others, trained there, did the hard work, overcame their fears and flew cross countries across the Alaska wilderness. All became excellent pilots - Alaska pilots.

As far as being mission oriented, take Susan Metcalf for instance. She was a warm, soft-spoken yet determined college student who wanted to learn to fly to get out to more of the outlying villages. Her primary goal was to teach Native American kids to swim. Drownings at the time were prevalent throughout Alaska. She wanted to make a difference and I believe she did that.

My first instrument student needed to get to and from his mining operation. By the way, on his graduation, he rewarded me with the "delicacy of the moose." It was a big old five pound chunk of liver!

My great friend Jerry Bagley, upon joining up with our flying club, aced his checkout. His landings were smooth and perfect. Pretty soon I began watching his techniques to pick up pointers.

I could also go on about all the different types of exotic aircraft and the pilots that flew them. An example would be pilots like Jay Harris who owned a beautiful Helio-Courier. Jay, a very successful businessman, knew of and had to get to a lot of great fishing spots. He was very good at landing on the numbers, stopping on the numbers and turning off at the approach end of the runway.

David Alton, one of my excellent instrument students, owned a beautiful Cessna 206 amphibian in which we spent a lot of time. What a great experience. I had some trouble with pulling the gear up before landing. Let's see, blue means water landing?

My point is there's a treasure trove of experience available through flight instructing in and around Anchorage. My advice is to take advantage of the situation and learn some additional skills while teaching additional ratings. If you become a good listener and a good student yourself you may pick up on one or two items that may save your life someday. Know and respect 'your' limitations and the limitations of your aircraft and of course, refuse to do anything dangerous or illegal.

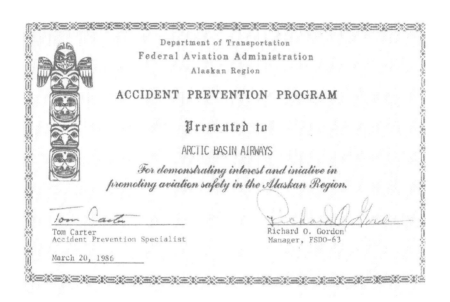

It's a good idea to have respect for and work closely with the Alaskan Region FAA. They have the back ground, experience and knowledge to provide guidance and safeguards in many areas of Alaska aviation.

Many of the rules and regulations we fly by have been the product of years of analysis of incidents and accidents.

The Alaska Airman's Safety Foundation and other groups provide a vast resource of safety information for pilots as well. Read all you can and associate with those groups.

When you're alone, hundreds of miles from anyone, it might be tempting to break a rule. Just remember, the rules are there for a reason. That is, to keep you and your passengers alive.

ABA Emblem on all our aircraft.

Now that you have a license to fly in Alaska, let's take off and do some flying and sightseeing around the nearby Anchorage Bowl areas. You might even find some good items to chunk into your experience storehouse.

CHAPTER 12

NORTHERN COOK INLET BASIN

I'd gotten a good taste of Alaska, hauling fish the first year and flight instructing through my first winter. The following spring and summer seasons were very educational as well. I especially got to know the Cook Inlet Basin area; well enough in fact, I knew where most of the wildlife hung out and where the most beautiful and spectacular scenic spots were.

The Anchorage Convention and Visitors Bureau gave us an award, 'Wild about Anchorage', for the handling of scenic tours. The award is based on tourist comments and feedback about the highlights of their visit. Thanks Anchorage and thank you folks, for taking the time to send in your comments. My greatest reward was the enjoyment I felt being a part of it all and opening the Alaskan wilderness doorway for a lot of new people.

Mount McKinley or 'Denali' as it is called by the natives of Alaska is about the most requested destination in Alaska. Standing tall at 20,300 feet, it gives one a sense of the vastness and beauty of the natural wilderness there. Of course, you want to see the mountain; however, there are lots of other things to see and places to visit in the area. I would highly recommend one or two scenic flights for anyone traveling to the Last Frontier.

Just around the corner from Anchorage you'll find the Knik Glacier. It's exciting to fly there and be very close to tons of ice grinding through the valley and to get a bird's eye view of the massive crevices in the ice.

Following the Knik River toward the Glacier and Lake George

The Knik (pronounced cah-nik) Glacier and Lake George, near Palmer, are both very dramatic and close to Anchorage. For aviators, I recommend a gradual climb out of Anchorage by way of Eagle River, Birchwood and the Eklutna Indian Reservation, then to remain south of Palmer and follow the Knik River to the glacier at altitude. You should be high enough to safely overfly the glacier and soon arrive in the Lake George area.

Approaching Lake George near the top of the Knik Glacier.

Once over the lake you can easily tour the Glacier coming down instead of climbing up. This provides a better safety margin and improves the comfort level for your passengers.

The photo above was actually taken from one of our S-Turns on the way down vs on the way up. Off to the right of the picture is a small canyon that may afford a good escape route in case of engine failure. At least the Glacier is lower on that side.

Believe it or not many aircraft have unintentionally landed on glaciers simply because they could not turn away or climb faster than the rising terrain. Climbing up a glacier is the same as climbing up a mountain side. The higher you get the more marginal your performance. Add in a little density altitude factor and / or turbulence and you drift over to the gambling side of life.

On our tours, after a turn or two over Lake George, we would begin a series of large gentle S-turns and proceeding down the glacier until reaching the glacier face.

One turn across the face from right to left will set you up to follow the river down at low level. This is about as close as you can get to being on the glacier without actually landing on it.

The razor sharp ice stands ready to rip your aircraft apart.

When flying over, you're looking down into deep crevices with what looks like razor sharp ice knives, all set up to rip your airplane into shreds. The blue-shaded ice crevices are filled with the bluest blue water you've ever seen. I've heard that the dense ice actually traps blue light rays inside which then transfers to the water at the bottom and the pools along the surface.

Although there are many spectacular sites, remember, if you're the pilot; please don't get caught up into sightseeing. Your primary obligation is to get your passengers and the aircraft back in one piece! I know of several that did not meet that obligation. There have been several fatal mid-air and terrain collisions that have occurred over this and other glaciers.

Orbiting animals within 25 miles of Anchorage is another very dangerous activity. It's a good idea for you as a passenger to be vigilant of your surroundings in either case and to tell the pilot if you notice any other aircraft in your area. To further enhance safety, several air tour destinations have their own recommended frequencies for pilot communication.

Speaking of glacier tours, let's talk about Mt. McKinley's famous Amphitheater, Devils Gorge and the Ruth Glacier.

Again, a gradual climb out of Anchorage is best. When you arrive at your maximum altitude, you can spend some great time in slow descending turns on your way down the mountain.

The Amphitheater is probably the most spectacular area of the mountain. Snow-laden rock spires surround you, appearing as giant monoliths. They protrude straight up into the blue sky and dive straight down into abyss-like canyons and are gigantic in proportion to anything you've ever seen before. I recommend at least one or two descending turns in the Amphitheater.

As you leave the amphitheater, you'll pass between two of these giant spires of granite, exiting through the Devils Gorge and arriving over the Ruth Glacier.

You can continue your slow descent following the Ruth and as you leave the mountain areas, you can continue low on toward Anchorage possibly observing various wildlife.

This trip is about twice as long as the Knik Glacier Tour but well worth the time.

As a pilot, in a non-pressurized aircraft, you should not descend faster than 500 feet per minute with passengers. As a passenger, you have the right to ask him or her to slow their descent if you're experiencing ear or sinus pain. It's also okay to question a pilot's approach to a mountain or a glacier. If they're headed directly toward a steep mountainside, or are at low level headed up from the face of a glacier, you might question that.

As a pilot, you need to check the winds aloft forecast to see where the smoothest conditions are. There were days when we refused to fly due to high winds aloft from a particular direction. Usually a 40 mph wind from the northwest would shut us down on McKinley.

Now, if you're really adventure minded, check out the glacier tour operators. They actually fly up and land with skis on the glacier. I understand landing on glaciers started in the 1930's. A fellow named Bob Reeve flying a Fairchild with wooden skis, flew up and landed on glaciers in the Valdez area. Don Shelton was another early explorer of the tradition. Flying out of Talkeetna, he transported climbers and gear onto the glaciers of Mt. McKinley. Today, flying in Alaska is tough. Can you imagine the challenges these early pioneers must have had?

If you're going to spend some time flying in Alaska, Anchorage and the Cook Inlet Basin area is a good place to begin where you can brush up on your skills or learn something from a local instructor or pilot. This area is somewhat protected by the Alaska Range and has been called the Banana Belt of Alaska. The moderate temperatures generally average 20 degrees in winter and 65 in summer. In a sense you're in an island environment and in order to get out of the Cook Inlet Basin you've got to go out the 'doors', mountain passes that are guarded by wind and weather. The only highway exits for driving out consist of one road north and one road south. The road north is the only road that one can follow all the way out of Alaska.

Most flight training is done out to the northwest, across the Knik Arm - a branch of the Cook Inlet and in and around the famous Mat-Su Valley.

Mat-Su Valley dairy farm with private landing strip

This mostly agricultural area is primarily flat with nice hay fields and straight roads which allows for great ground reference training maneuvers as well as emergency procedure practice.

Here in the Mat-Su Valley your training can be accomplished with a back drop of the Alaska Range anchored by Mount McKinley and Mount Foraker.

Can you imagine doing Lazy 8's and Chandelles (both commercial training maneuvers) with the snow covered 20,000 foot peak as your reference point? It's absolutely awesome. If you're a student or already a commercial pilot visiting Alaska, you need to grab a local instructor and work on your commercial maneuvers out there.

Ever heard of Mt. Foraker? This magnificent mountain has been generally overshadowed by the more popular McKinley. However, both mountains are very close to the same height! In fact, Mt. Foraker is so much like Mt. McKinley that it was accidently climbed by a group who realized, to their chagrin, what they'd done after they reached the summit of the wrong mountain. Can you imagine the feeling, the swing from euphoria to defeat, standing there, weather worn, fatigued, beaten and gazing across a 20 mile wide abyss at your intended goal?

My hat's off to them. Most have no idea what it takes to climb a 20,000 foot mountain. These guys did it and, I'm sure some or all went on to climb McKinley at a later time.

The Chugach Range, being the closest range to Anchorage, is a great training area for mountain and pass flying. The range runs north and south along the inlet. The passes are quite beautiful, challenging and close to home. Be sure to only work these passes, or any passes in Alaska, in decent weather. 3,000 foot ceilings and 15 miles visibility are pretty good numbers for most of them. Blue sky is better, of course.

Within the Anchorage area are some other obvious mountains such as the Sleeping Lady (Mt. Susitna) and Mt. Redoubt. From there begins the totally awesome volcanic mountains of the Aleutian Range.

For wildlife viewing, you might try the Mt Susitna area generally teaming with wild life. One day while flying, we counted 24 black bears on the mountain. The bears didn't pay any attention to us and were apparently feasting on berries. If you decide to observe wild life or take photographs, make darn sure one is assigned to do so and one of you is designated the pilot of the aircraft, looking ahead.

Again, if you're a pilot, conducting a scenic tour of any kind, remember the scenery is for your passengers, not for you! As mentioned, this beautiful spectacular scenery and wildlife has caused many accidents and deaths around the Cook Inlet Basin.

There are several airports in the area surrounding Anchorage. Birchwood, Palmer, Wasilla and Talkeetna, are other cities just north of Anchorage that have airports. All have paved runways and are popular for training flights from Anchorage however be aware of aircraft operating with no radios at those airports.

"Your primary obligation as a pilot is to see and avoid terrain, other aircraft and inescapable situations!"

"Always... Always... Always... Leave Yourself an Out!"

Another popular attraction for your first bush strip training flight could be Skweentna. The Skweentna Lodge provides a great wilderness setting and is located at the confluence of the Yetna and Skweentna Rivers, 50 miles southwest of Talkeetna. The lodge owners are very friendly and hospitable. Be sure and bring your fishing pole! They have great food and do guided fishing and hunting trips. After flying in there, to get to the lodge, plan a good 75 yard hike or call ahead for a ride on a four wheeler. If hiking, carry a weapon and make plenty of noise. This is wilderness and bear country!

"This is awfully big country for such a little airplane."

According to FAA regulations, we have to send our students on cross-country flights in order to attain their Private or Commercial Pilot's License. Considering that the Anchorage

Bowl area is bordered on the east by the Chugach Mountains, on the north by the Talkeetna Mountains, to the west by the Alaska Range and an awesome string of volcanoes (the beginning of the Aleutian Range) and to the south by the Cook Inlet, students have to be pretty top notch pilots to do a 300 mile solo cross country. It gets even trickier in the winter when there's less daylight and sudden weather with winds easily increasing to 50 or 60 mph at 2,000 feet above the surface. An un-forecast wind increase in the Lower Forty Eight may only be an inconvenience, but in Alaska, it can be deadly. Most of our students did their cross country flights in Cessna 152's, which many of you know are two seat, low horsepower trainers. Of course, the instructor has to go with each of the students on a few trips to check out their judgment, navigation and landing skills. A lost student in Alaska takes on a whole different meaning than in the lower Forty Eight.

Through the years, we developed all types of advanced flight training programs for our commercial level and higher students. A primary skill was pass flying. We not only taught them the practicalities of pass flying but journeyed through actual passes with them.

Inside A Mountain Pass on a C.A.V.U. day.

To the north of Anchorage several passes are located within range of training aircraft, the closest being Independence Mine Pass. This small pass leads up and around the famous Independence Mine. If it's warm be aware of your aircraft performance along this route, where density altitude played a role in at least one fatal crash I know of. Other passes exiting through the Talkeetna Mountains lead to Glen Allen and Fairbanks. The Alaska Range and other passes leading out of the Cook Inlet Basin area are discussed more thoroughly in future chapters.

Pass Flying can be somewhat of a challenge depending on time
of day and weather.

Let's take a look to the south of Anchorage, where we send
our students many times on their initial cross country trips.
Flights to Soldotna, Kenai or Homer, with the exception of having
to cross the Turnagain Arm, are over some decent terrain and are
generally the safest cross-country trips you can take from
Anchorage.

CHAPTER 13

SOUTHERN COOK INLET BASIN

If you proceed south out of the Anchorage area you'll cross over the famous Turnagain Arm. This arm of the Cook Inlet was named Turnagain following Captain Cook's famous turnaround in 1819. I could name a couple of fiords in the Prince William Sound 180 Fiords for the same exact reason. Many look alike. Most have dead end canyons.

After crossing Turnagain, you will be over the Kenai Peninsula. This peninsula is bordered by the arm on the north, the Cook Inlet west and the Gulf of Alaska on the south and east. It's connected to the mainland by only three miles of terrain. That's pretty close to being an island I'd say!

The cities of Kenai, Soldotna and Homer, on the Kenai Peninsula all have paved runways and facilities.

There's a beautiful bay at Homer that makes this flight spectacular. The Kachemak Bay is a beautiful place, with four or five glaciers feeding into the bay. And, just on the far side of the bay nestled in the coves of the Bay and the Gulf, are the villages of English Bay, Port Graham and Seldovia. Some of these original

Russian colonies are still inhabited by traditional, Russian-speaking citizens. These beautiful seaport towns are very interesting and worth visiting. All of them have histories dating to the mid1800's. None of the runways are suitable for students.

Seward, a seaport town and the beginning point of the Iditarod Trail, lies on the south coast of the peninsula. It has a nice airport, but is an undesirable destination for students due to the pass flying required and the high vertical mountains surrounding the airport. However, Seward is a good destination to teach pass flying. I always thoroughly enjoyed flying through Resurrection Pass which begins near the old gold mining town of Hope on the Turnagain Arm and continues to the Gulf of Alaska at Seward.

A more scenic and challenging trip from Anchorage to Seward is to fly directly south from Anchorage. Stay west of the Chugach Range to Skilak Lake, turn left (eastbound) and follow the lake, bearing north-northeast as you approach the upper end. You continue northbound now to follow the Kenai River Gorge. Keep my glacier, 'Priest Glacier', off your right wing as you head north. As you pass Bear Mountain or Russian mountain, proceed back eastbound when terrain and ceiling are adequate. At that point, you can connect with Resurrection Pass southbound. You travel over Lower Russian Lake and Upper Russian Lake as you follow the pass. You'll eventually come up on the Resurrection River which you follow to Exit Glacier (where else would you expect?) Turn the corner to the south and the magnificent seaport town of Seward and the Gulf of Alaska will open up to you. Although I developed this route through necessity, it turned out to be about the most scenic route I'd ever taken. It's an unforgettable experience and well worth the time and effort.

Many times, low ceilings along the northeastern Kenai Peninsula obscured all the pass entrances, whereas the Skilak southern route usually had a good ceiling. A good cloud base indicator for this route is the ceiling report at Seward. A 4,000 foot ceiling there, with 10 miles visibility, no precipitation and an increasing temperature dew-point spread, along with a good forecast, would be desirable.

In this pass, be sure to stay well ahead of your aircraft and leave yourself an out. Keep to the right, leave room to make a 180 at all times. There are only a couple of wide turnaround points along this route. Anywhere else is going to be a very tight turn at best.

If you decide to try this route, be sure to take someone along who's been through there. Also make sure you have proper charts and mark them well to find your turns. I would suggest flying this route under clear blue skies the first couple of times.

In summer, there's one area along the way where water blows out the side of a mountain 75 to 100 feet horizontally into a small lake with more waterfalls dropping into the river. The view is spectacular! By the way, there are no roads in this pass. The area is total wilderness.

Other than the passes to Seward, there's another pass well known to most Alaska aviators and that is Portage Pass leading to the City of Whittier and the Prince William Sound. Located on the north end of the Kenai Peninsula, the infamous Portage Pass has more airplane wreckage in it than any pass in the world! As I've said in the past, some days you are in a wonderland of pristine beauty and on other days you don't want to be there.

Watch the weather carefully no matter which pass you fly. Portage Pass is located adjacent to Portage Glacier, just beyond the lake and opens the doorway to the Prince William Sound.

The City of Whittier, located on the east coast of the peninsula and on the Prince William Sound also has an airport which is not recommended for any student. The airport has a short one-way runway with high terrain on one end and ocean waters on the other and has dangerous fast changing conditions.

Whittier Airport in November

About the only person I've known to land on the runway with winds coming out of the pass was my friend, Bob Jones. He'd about had it with a very irritating, arrogant, flight examiner, who had constantly gone beyond the normal boundaries of check ride protocol. Bob initially refused when instructed to make a short field landing there. He knew better, however, the examiner chided him for not being able to land under the gusty conditions.

"Okay, here we go." Bob sighed.

Although the conditions were very gusty, he made a beautiful landing, taxied into the run-up area and shut the engine down.

The examiner, puzzled, exclaimed, "What the heck are you doing?"

Bob said, "I told you I could land here... Didn't say I could take off."

As they got out of the airplane, the examiner had his clipboard in hand, "Okay, you passed. What's your plan?"

Bob shrugged, "Helicopter?"

The examiner continued to check off the various tasks and with a changed attitude, "Awe, let's get a ride over to Whittier, have some lunch. Maybe the wind will die down. I'd sure like to get back to Anchorage before five."

After a good halibut lunch and a short wait, the winds indeed died down. They had a good flight back to Anchorage. I'm not sure if Bob just wanted a free lunch or what.

One winter, on the commuter route to Valdez, I flew over the runway for several weeks, glancing down at a C-152 flipped on its' back. It seems a couple of guys attempted a landing on the snow covered runway and didn't realize the depth of the snow. It doesn't take a lot of snow to flip over a wheel aircraft. I heard that no one was injured but that's got to be an embarrassing way to leave your aircraft.

Speaking of winter, Whittier can be a virtual ghost town at times. As a matter of fact, this old World War II Submarine base becomes very quiet with not much going on around the docks. In the dead of winter, the closest meal you can get is located away from the water closer to the mountain side of town. There's a local restaurant located above a bar with the best beer battered halibut I've ever tasted. The cook and the people are wonderful. However, best keep an eye on the thousand pound icicles hanging from the roof. Personally, I like Whittier better in the summer.

Ken 'Clint' Albright - Pilot – Adventurer in Whittier, Alaska

Back along the western shores of the Kenai Peninsula on the Cook Inlet lie some of the best clam digs in the world. The best beaches for razor clams are between Clam Gulch and Ninilchik. Some of the beaches are landable but occasionally full of surprises. A lot of folks fly down for the day, get a good bucket of the huge clams, then fly home and have a great party.

90

I recommend flying down with someone who's been there several times before trying it on your own.

One thing to remember, even though you're only 30 minutes from Anchorage, <u>Do not get complacent about survival equipment</u>. Be ready to survive - alone, with no help from anyone. People meet their Maker all the time along the Cook Inlet, many within sight of Anchorage.

Turnagain Arm of the Cook Inlet at low tide.

Two of the best Alaska helicopter pilots I knew, both Vietnam Vets, had a forced landing in their helicopter just across the Turn-again Arm from Anchorage. After waiting several hours, they decided to hike out, "just over to Hope."

Hope is a small, remote, recovering gold mining town on the Cook Inlet. I say remote, but it's within binocular range across the Inlet from Anchorage. Well, three days later, after continual problems dealing with bears, living on berries and nuts and just barely surviving, they limped into town. The irony is that their helicopter was found the day after their forced landing. I'm sure someone learned a good lesson there. They survived their ordeal but could have just as easily not survived. I'm sure the frustrating part was knowing that Anchorage was always in sight just across that deadly little stretch of water.

While we're in the area here's another note of advice. Stay off the beaches in the northern Cook Inlet and the adjacent arms. The sandy beaches can turn to quicksand in a matter of minutes and with the tidal movements the quicksand can suddenly turn into concrete. People have been trapped, lost limbs, or lost their lives due to this phenomenon. Tides in the general area have been recorded up to 40 feet and generally average in the mid 30'S.

I've flown over and watched the 'Boar Tide', sometimes 30 to 40 feet, come rolling in up the Turnagain Arm. The Boar Tide is a solid wave of water and is very awesome to watch; however, it's not something you want to see coming at you from the water or the beach. Don't let those wind-surfing guys fool you into thinking its safe out there. They are pros and can read the situation very well. I put those guys in the same category as bungee jumpers, sky base jumpers and other high risk activities. The water's ice cold and the sand can kill you.

If driving, there are some great turnouts along the road to Portage where you can easily view the Boar Tide rushing in. Just stay off the mud flats.

Ever been clamming? Here's one for the books.

Tom Milton, a good friend and fellow pilot, along with his friend, Jeff Barger, flew a Cessna 180 down the inlet to do some clam digging. They had a big Alaska clam bake planned for the evening back in Anchorage. Jeff had been down there several times. This was Tom's first experience.

The flight was only 35 minutes from Anchorage to landing on the beach. The flight and landing were nice and uneventful.

Tom got a quick check-out on clamming and was fairly successful. However, after a couple of hours in the mud, he decided he'd had enough. He waded out into the water to rinse off some of the worst mud and dirt, gazed around at the majestic scenery and began to stroll down the beach. He picked up a few shells and rocks and skipped them across the water.

Realizing he'd wandered about a hundred yards from the airplane, he decided to head back. As he turned, out of the corner of his eye, he caught a movement further down the beach. He put some of the best shells in his pocket and continued to walk toward the small, dark creature at the water's edge.

"Hmmm...."he said to himself, "looks interesting. Wonder what it is - a porcupine or maybe a badger."

He felt for his camera while watching the animal, hoping he wouldn't lose sight of it. After he'd walked about another 25 yards, he suddenly realized that the shoreline went on forever and perhaps his view had been somewhat distorted. He also realized that what he thought was a small animal was actually a large bear a long way down the beach. He turned around and headed for his airplane, his gun and his friend. He glanced back and saw the bear running at full speed toward him, grunting and snarling. He bolted as fast as he could towards the airplane. He had no weapon with him and after about a minute, realized he probably was not going to beat the bear to the plane.

He was running as hard as he physically could when a different sound, other than his own loud breathing and pounding heart, began to penetrate his ears. The faraway voice seemed to be carrying in the wind, whistling through his ears. Then, it began sounding more like yelling. Although he couldn't quite understand what was being yelled, it seemed to be repeating itself. The noise of the bear's breath and grunts were blending with his own now. The thumping of his own heartbeat was now pounding in his ears. In a surreal world now, he knew the bear was closing on him.

Then, with the bear within 50 feet, he suddenly understood what the person was yelling.

"Stttttooopppppp Ruunnnnninnnggggg!!!! Stttttooopppppp Ruunnnnninnnggggg!!!!"

Tom knew he was dead anyway, so he slid to a stop, spun around to face the bear. Screaming, he threw up his arms. The bear, a large brown bear, now within 20 feet, put the brakes on, slinging sand, gravel and slobber all over Tom. Tom stood his ground. His sudden action added to his screaming totally surprised the bear. He continued yelling and throwing rocks at the bear which by now had headed toward the tree line. If Tom hadn't stopped and stood his ground, he wouldn't have survived.

Tom slowly turned and on wobbly legs, walked the remaining 20 feet to the airplane, sat down on the wheel and leaned forward resting his head on his folded arms. Jeff walked up, opened the cargo door and swung a heavy bucket of clams in.

"Tom... You alright?" Jeff asked.

"Oh, yeah," he said... "You 'bout ready to go?"

"Yeah. We've got plenty of clams and a nice bear story for our clam bake tonight," his friend replied.

"Jeff, I've never had so much fun clam digging. Did I scare you bringing my bear up here to the plane?" Tom asked.

They both chuckled and began gathering their gear. Tom slapped his friend on the back. As Jeff turned around, Tom extended his hand.

As they shook hands, he said, "Jeff, Thanks for saving my life."

"I'm glad it worked out Tom," Jeff said.

As they began to taxi down the beach for takeoff, they saw a new bear with two cubs ambling up the beach.

"You know, that combination there might not have worked out so well," Jeff remarked.

Tom nodded in agreement and then spun the 180 Cessna around for takeoff, putting the bears in his rear view mirror so to speak. He made a rolling check of the mags, then gave the engine full power. The engine sounded good... Everything was in the green. Now, here's the part where you hope nothing goes wrong. Spending a night or two on this particular beach is not that attractive.

They lifted off the beach and began their climbing turn to gain some altitude to get across the inlet.

"High enough for you?" asked Tom.

"Yeah. Let's go to Anchorage. Nice sunset," Jeff said.

As the sun eased lower on the horizon, they began to pick up the lights of civilization. Now, along with the feeling of relief, fatigue began to set in.

Jeff said, "Gonna be a great clambake. Who's coming?"

"We are," Tom replied.

They both laughed.

While on the subject of running from bears I would like to tell you a standing bush pilot joke that will probably survive forever.

A group of fishermen chartered a C-206 to fly them to a remote fishing spot. They were geared up with the best equipment - boots, mosquito nets, the works. When the pilot showed up, the fishermen noticed he was wearing tennis shoes.

"What the heck are you doing wearing tennis shoes?" asked one of the fishermen.

"Well, sir, that's in case of a bear attack."

"Bear attack? Har!... Har!... Har!... That's got to be the stupidest thing I've ever heard! I thought you were a bush pilot! You don't seem to know anything about the bush! Now I've read a lot about bears and I know one thing, you cannot outrun a bear!"

The bush pilot contemplated and rubbed his chin.

"Well, Sir, that may be true, but, actually, I only have to outrun you."

In truth, although the joke is somewhat funny and was probably a good comeback, the actual tactic probably would not work. Oh, it might work on a black bear, but a grizzly or brownie would simply go to the next person. Black Bears will eat you, always fight them. Brownies and Grizzlies just want to kill you because you're moving... Best to play dead.

Actually, if you want to see bears up close and in their natural habitat, take the McNeil River Tour. The mouth of the McNeil River isn't far from Anchorage and is located on the west side of the Cook Inlet just across from Homer, Alaska. The Cook Inlet Basin is home to thousands of bears consisting of several varieties. Beware, if you get off the beaten path for any reason. Occasionally when you're on the beaten path, you may also be susceptible to problems with bears. Maulings and deaths have occurred in and around the Anchorage area and throughout the Cook Inlet basin.

The Turnagain Arm looking east toward Portage Glacier

Are you ready for some real wilderness flying? Okay then, let's go to the Alaska Outback, get out of the bowl and away from the Cook Inlet.

CHAPTER 14

'OUTBACK' ALASKA

Throughout a couple of great years at ABA Flying Club, we had a lot of students graduate to higher license and ratings as well as visited a lot of Alaska. Personally, I had gained a lot of experience through flying with and being around a lot of highly experienced guys.

Somewhere near the end of summer in 1986 we heard news about a possible oil price crash. However, it didn't hit home until one Saturday morning when only a couple of students showed up. I personally had nothing scheduled but came in during the day to check on things. 'Nothing in the morning at all, hmmm... At least Buck's got a couple of students this afternoon.'

A few minutes later, Buck tapped on my office door and stuck his head in, "Tone, I'm heading home. My last student just cancelled. Things aren't looking too good... Nothing much on the schedule next week either."

"OK, Buck," I responded, "I'll give you a call if something comes up."

No matter how hard we tried over the next few weeks, times had gone bad in Anchorage. Very few students were scheduling flights for training.

I remember one of our pilots saying, "Tony, the way things are going, there's going to be a lot of big boy toys scattered all over the hillsides."

Sure enough, it happened, no one was flying for recreation. It was as if the final curtain had fallen on the good times theater. There were lots of disappointed people at Arctic Basin Airways, including myself. However, there's a time and place for everything and I suppose you might say that Arctic Basin Airways Flying Club was a wonderful happening and hopefully many were left with good memories of those days.

Out of necessity, I, like the other flight instructors, began the task of looking for other work. At least by this time, I had built up my Alaska flight hours and gained some more knowledge and experience.

After a few days of searching, I wandered into Wilbur's; a family owned and operated charter company and flight school. My first impression was that they ran a professional aviation business. The reception area was very large, neat and clean, with all the right stuff around. Terri Mitchell, the receptionist was very helpful and friendly. After talking with her and one of the flight instructors at the counter, they sent me to a back office to meet with Rich Wilbur, the Chief Pilot. I found him to be congenial but very down to business. He liked my resume and made me a job offer by the end of the interview, pending a background check and so on.

Of course, this is just the beginning of getting on line with any company. There's a lot of training and testing required which takes time. However, to begin earning some money, he sent me to their chief flight instructor. After a thorough checkout, I went to work there as a flight instructor and soon began working my way up to becoming a line pilot with Wilbur's, 'The Family Airline'.

Wilbur's Cessna 402 aircraft.

CHAPTER 15

WILBUR'S, THE FAMILY AIRLINE

Joe and Anne Wilbur, along with their three sons, Rich, Steve and Bruce, owned and managed the operation. All were very good at their jobs and ran a tight ship. Rich served as Chief Pilot and Check Airman, Steve as Director of Operations and Bruce as Director of Maintenance.

Through the years, the Wilbur family had developed one of the busiest air carriers in Alaska and developed a virtual life line to some of the most remote locations in the region.

This is also where I met a lifelong friend, Steve Doty. Steve turned out to be one of the best mechanics I'd ever worked with. He was an awesome mechanic – Best of the Best.

Also guys like Alan Carson, Tom Milton, John Robertson, Mark Craig, Wayne Brockman, Keith Walbert and Dan Lentz, all were great pilots and together, we helped build the company into a dynamic commuter airline.

In the beginning, I worked with a few students as well as took various scenic tours and charters. Flying charters, I found, was a little different type of flying with a mix of cargo and clientele. We were moving everything from concrete to chickens, dogs, fuel, groceries, engines, parts, everything you could imagine a remote village or mining operation would need.

The clientele included people from all walks of life, from locals of the many scattered villages, to doctors, troopers, prisoners, environmentalists, seismologists, cooks with supplies, miners, patients and on occasion, military personnel including officers.

As you've probably determined by now, this is not a book necessarily about me and my adventures. I really want to try to somehow give you an understanding of the total picture of a place and time that has passed. If I had a list of the folks who flew with us at Wilbur's, I would include them by name here. You were a courageous bunch of folks! It takes intestinal fortitude to climb into a Seneca II, Cessna 402, or a B99 Airliner headed into the wilderness of Alaska.

Things eventually began to develop from a charter business into flying a mix of more structured scheduled runs. From Cessna 402's, we graduated into the Beech 99 Airliners. Wilbur's was very good at moving a pilot up the ranks after they had proven themselves. Many of us continued our careers into flying turbo props and jets, some on to heavy jets with major airlines.

The following chapter involves some of the most memorable places and events of that period.

Onward and upward I began my most hazardous flying. These were flight missions of a more serious nature. Getting supplies or people in or out could and occasionally did mean life or death. These life-line flights followed invisible highways, precariously weaving through rock and ice, smoke and fire, in total wilderness.

CHAPTER 16

McGRATH

One of my first experiences with Wilbur's was on a charter from Anchorage to McGrath. This route took me completely across the impressive Alaskan Range. On the way, I noticed the flawless blue sky above and that the air was as smooth as glass. As I looked around me, I saw snowcapped, rocky peaks appearing to go on forever.

I eventually and abruptly came to the edge of the Alaska Range, departed the strong vertical peaks of the mountains and began a gradual descent into the magnificent tundra area toward McGrath.

Now I was feeling a sigh of relief to at least have a place to land in an emergency. However, not one sign of civilization appeared during the next one hundred miles which brought home the realization that I was truly on my own should that occur. 'I'll have some good firepower on my next trip out... You betcha!'

As I approached the McGrath airport I could see the wide Kuskokwim River which made a winding turn up and around the airport and city. Except for a small land section to the southeast McGrath is completely surrounded by the river giving it an island appearance.

The wind was out of the north and as I worked my way down, I realized the end of runway 34 was right at the river, a wide icy cold river filled with ice flows. Down low over the river, I glanced downward for a second and made a mental note never to land short! Other than that, I was lined up on a snow covered runway.

The landing event worked out fine with a soft touchdown and surprisingly good braking. After landing, I taxied quickly toward the largest group of buildings at the airport. I pulled up and shut down next to a plane with skis. I didn't see any tie-downs, so I simply closed the door and began walking over toward the terminal building. The air was quite crisp, about 10 degrees with blue sky above. Suddenly a slipping sound came from behind me. I spun around and to my surprise, a dog sled came quietly driving by. The musher was Native American, had on a heavy fur lined parka type outfit and looked plenty warm. He pulled in to the terminal also, dropped anchor, pulled off his parka and drooped it over the sled. He nodded and smiled and went inside. His team, quiet, well-behaved, sat down and began waiting patiently.

As I approached the dogs and sled, I had the feeling I'd really arrived in the real Alaska. His dogs were beautiful, looking much like the Alaskan Huskies you would see in "Sergeant Preston of the Yukon," a great TV show somewhere back in my childhood. I'd best refer to "Snow Dogs" for you younger generation. Later on I found out that the dog teams and sleds were somewhat more dependable than snow machines in the incredible sub-zero temperatures.

As I entered the very rustic terminal building, I noticed first and foremost, a nice fire going in the large fireplace. Of course, I made a beeline for the heat. Other than glad to be inside, I really didn't know what to expect. Then a cheerful voice echoed across the room.

"You must be Tony."

"Sure am, Laura?"

"Laura Gardner, station manager... How about some coffee or soup?"

Laura turned out to be a great agent and a wonderful friend who saw us through thick and thin during those Wilbur's years.

After a couple of generous cups of strong coffee I had some additional time to kill, so I decided to take a walk and check out the rest of the town.

Laura pointed me in the direction of the center of town. I thanked her for the coffee and stepped outside. I took a good look across the airport area. 'Yep lots of snow, frozen river, quiet.'

I walked over to a small street, passed a couple of closed up buildings, then saw a sign. 'F.A.A. Weather'. Entering, I saw the counter with some various publications stacked neatly. Jim was sitting at a small desk buried in some manuals.

As he looked up, I spoke. "Hello, Tony Priest, just flew in a little bit ago. How are you doing?"

"Great, can I help you?"

"Just checking on the weather and just wondering where I'd find the main part of town."

"Town? Where'd you come from just now?"

"Just walked over from the terminal building."

Jim chuckled, "Well, you just walked through the middle of town!" As it turned out, Laura's was about the most going place in McGrath at the time.

I flew in and out of McGrath many times through the winter and eventually had a unique, cold weather incident that bears relating.

By this time, the general rule I'd established for myself was to do everything right and simply stay alive. However, as I found out, occasionally, certain events or phenomenon may occur that slip you a little further out, closer to the edge.

This event occurred at McGrath during my first winter there.

On that January day, I began to amend my basic rule with more specific numbers.

I knew it was cold as I approached McGrath. It was a bright sunny day, with ice-fog drifting in the valleys. Small columns of smoke were rising from the houses then settling downward.

As I descended into the river valley, I observed the temperature gauge plummeting well below zero. I had seen and knew that occasionally it was quite colder in the valleys. However, this was my first experience with such a radical swing in temperature. From 3,000 feet, I had a temperature change of more than 75 degrees. I had gone from + 30 to - 45 degrees in a matter of minutes. Yes, things began to fog up.

An inversion, as in inverse, backwards, was the culprit weather phenomenon causing all the problems.

The normal temperature lapse rate is two degrees Celsius, or three and one-half degrees Fahrenheit, per 1,000 feet of altitude. It's supposed to decrease as you ascend, not as you descend! What happens to cause this dreaded phenomena is that a warmer air mass settles over the cold air and traps it in the valleys and at low levels. It quickly begins to cause problems not only for airmen, but for everyone on the ground as well.

As I touched down the tires squeaked on the snow covered runway. I quickly headed for the terminal, planning for a quick turnaround. I knew my clock was ticking as I eased the mixtures back shutting off the engines.

As soon as I shut off the mags, I reset the mixtures to full rich and moved the throttles to start position as well. The reason is that things break. Throttle and mixture cables may get stuck wherever you leave them. On one occasion around - 40, I opened up my heavy duty headset, only to have it break in half. I quickly learned to place my headset over my knee until it was flexible and warm enough to place on my head.

This particular day, my outbound passengers were delayed about "15 or 20 minutes." I quickly wrapped the insulated covers over the still warm engines.

After 25 minutes I realized my passengers may be having trouble themselves getting to the airport. I made a couple of phone calls and as suspected, my passengers were not going to make it out.

I quickly put on my gear, grabbed the mail, headed on to the plane. The covers were frozen solid like boards and hard to remove. Got it done and threw them into the cabin.

As I switched on the master, I glanced at the oil temp gauge. 'No temp... It's cold!'

Dropping my headset over my knee, I knew I would have one chance to start. I was banking on residual heat in the core of the engine and figured once started; I would be good to go.

After some careful priming, I pressed the starter. The engine roared to life right away. 'Now the other... No problem... Great, two good starts. OK! I'm out of here.'

I let the engines run at idle for about five minutes. Oil pressure had risen into the green; temps were still in the caution area.

After breaking loose from the ice, I slowly began to taxi out. Another five minutes had passed during taxi. 'Great, temps are just inside the edge of the green arc.' The outside air temperature gauge read - **47**.

Reaching the end of the runway, as a natural habit I turned the nose wheel to the right to begin a run-up on the right engine. This helps hold you in position instead of slipping on the ice. Everything looked good. After a similar process and a good check on the left engine, I taxied onto the runway. The oil temperature appeared to barely be in the edge of the green.

I lined up and added power slowly until I could no longer get traction with the brakes. A quick check on the gauges, I continued my takeoff. A few hundred feet and I was airborne. What performance!

'Gear up. Looks normal.'

'Out of 500 feet, oil temp's coming up'.

'Great... Not Great.' Both oil temps were continuing to rise. Oil pressure looks lower, not higher.

'Not good Not good...' as I 'bent' the airplane steeply to the left.

'Not going into the river!'

Oil temps were now going into redline, oil pressure was dropping. Temps were not stopping - well over redline now. Oil pressures bottom of the green.

'Gotta put this turkey on the ground!'

As I got into position for landing again, I began to ease back on the throttles, estimating if they quit, I would still make the runway.

Reducing the power further, I cleared the frozen river which could get you on either end of the runway. Touching down, I breathed a sigh of relief, thanked my Guardian Angel...again and taxied to parking.

After shutdown I went looking for a mechanic. Not much luck there, but after a while, one of the local pilots came over with a Red Devil. A Red Devil is basically a ducted propane heater with a strong blower.

After checking oil level and looking around the engine, things looked normal. We ran the end of the ducts underneath the engine and secured them inside the cowling. After a few tries, we had the heater fired up. We took off running for the terminal.

When you get below about minus 30, the cold begins to hurt. Below 40, it becomes downright painful to breathe, especially through your nose. Ski masks seem to work pretty well when accompanied by hats, scarves, a parka and ski pants along with two pair of gloves and minus 50 boots. Tricky to fly that way, but it's better than freezing.

After warming up a bit, I called in and discussed the situation with Steve, our chief mechanic. It was concluded I had an oil congealing problem in the oil filter. He advised me to superheat the engine and before another attempt, do another thorough run-up. He planned to take a good look at the problem on my return.

The situation was that the extreme cold had done its' thing on my aircraft, even with both engines at full takeoff power. Had I continued, both engines would have frozen up eventually, not from cold but from heat! Hard to imagine I suppose. My choice was to shut down and possibly save two good engines and possibly end up at the bottom of the river, or blow up two engines on the downwind, in position for landing. Hmmm. Let me think.

As it turned out, the engines were fine. The Red Devil did its' job. Both engines were toasty warm when we pulled the covers. After a normal start, quick taxi and good run up, I was headed home. It felt good to clear the hills and be up and out of the valley. As I glanced back at McGrath, I could see the ice crystals in the air, once again flocking the trees. What a winter wonderland.

As my thoughts turned to home, I turned on the autopilot and began taking off some of my outlandish outerwear... Wanted to look stylish getting out in Anchorage, the center of the Banana Belt. It was a toasty 22 degrees at Merrill Field.

On the way home, I decided to make Minus 40 degrees Fahrenheit my personal limitation number, or cutoff for flying.

Later on, I may have slipped past that on occasion, but only for med-evacs or other emergencies.

CHAPTER 17

NIKOLAI

Nikolai is a small remote village located north east of McGrath and north of the Alaska Range and was the nearest village to McGrath. We were in and out of there practically every day.

If you're coming through Merrill Pass in the Alaskan Range headed north, you're making a beeline for Nikolai. It sits adjacent to the Kuskokwim River and along a segment of the very famous Iditarod trail.

Again, this episode occurred in the middle of winter, February. No one had made it into the village for a week due to low ceilings, fog, ice and snow. The word was the folks really needed supplies and a couple of others really needed to get out.

On this particular day low ceilings persisted with snow showers throughout the area. With a week of heavy snow, all the terrain was white, white, white!

Things looked promising on this day as I broke out of the dark clouds over McGrath. The ceiling was about 2,000 feet.

Visibility was three to five miles with light snow showers. The temperature on the ground was about - 25 degrees.

At first glance, these conditions didn't seem to present any problem for me as I'd been to Nikolai many times before. My Cessna 402 was specially equipped with a full de-ice and anti-ice system which included of course, wing boots, tail boots, inboard boots, heated pitot static system, hot props, heated windshield and pressurized magnetos.

Needless to say I had a full aircraft, a Cessna 402B, with eight guys, all their gear along with mail and supplies. The load wasn't a problem. There was more danger in over-boosting the engines on takeoff than running out of runway. I believe Joe Wilbur was correct in that assumption. He was generally right most of the time when it came to getting around safely in the bush.

After a static filled phone call, I understood that they had been working to clear the runway for hours and it was finally suitable for landing. Visibility was generally three miles and the ceiling was about 1,500 feet. They would be extremely happy if I could get in. Frank Petrosky, the Chief of the Village, was also the Postmaster at the time and related they were low on supplies and had a lot of mail to go out.

From McGrath to Nikolai was less than 50 miles. However, with no GPS equipment available in those days and with no navaid signal at low level, one had to utilize their best skills of pilotage navigation. It's just about a lost art today. Pilotage consists of calculating time, speed, distance, observing landmarks, calculating wind correction angles, etc.

Takeoff was normal off the north runway. I circled around over the field just to make sure I had a perfect course to Nikolai when I departed McGrath. I was happy to see the ceiling had lifted slightly and visibility had improved.

I picked up the on course radial of the VOR, set in my wind correction angle and leveled off at two thousand feet. At about forty miles as expected, the nav flag popped up, showing I was no longer receiving a usable navigation signal.

Visibility was holding at about three to four miles now, however the snow showers along with the snow covered ground were beginning to create a precarious situation.

Remaining on the instruments a lot, I continually calculated my ETA to Nikolai. My usual landmarks were now blending in with the snow. The lakes and river, generally the most prominent features were now not only frozen, but snow covered. Keeping a watchful eye on the instruments, I was continually scanning for a landmark. None appeared. Now very close to white-out conditions, I was watching out for that little devil, Vertigo as snow began falling again.

'Times Up! Where's the village? Left - Right - ahead? Could I have missed it? Snowing more now. Where's that village! No smoke. Nothing but snow and ice everywhere.' By this time I had slowed down, straining to see some sign. 'Nothing!' Time to turn around. I glanced over my shoulder to let the guys know I must have missed the village and was planning to return to McGrath if I did not find it soon. As I glanced back, all the passengers were looking over their left shoulder. Every one!

Without speaking, I gently began a bank to the left making a 180 degree turn, rolling out at approximately where the guys had been looking. Suddenly in the mist, I saw a plume of smoke rising.

We were only two miles from the village.

'Now to find the runway'... I flew directly to the small plume of smoke and began picking out some structures in the large mounds of snow. I buzzed the village easing the props forward slightly and banked around to over-fly the runway.

As I did so, I could see snow machines, dog sleds and people coming out of their houses to meet the airplane. Everyone was converging toward the ramp area. It was an awesome sight and an incredible feeling to be a part of that. I sobered up from being all that as I began to realize the runway was as hard to see as the village was. I knew I had another intense job to do. That was to land this fully loaded airplane on a snow covered bush strip with very little visual cues to go by.

I kept close to the airport, dropping my gear on the downwind and full flaps on base leg. We utilized all our drag at these temperatures in order to keep our engines powered up and warm. The approach was half instrument, half visual. It was hard to discern the end of the runway but as I got lower and closer, I began to pick up snow covered buildings and obstacles that gave better depth perception.

Finally, with the stall warning coming on and off, the wheels silently touched the snow. Aerodynamically the airplane was through flying. I began carefully braking and found I had good traction. Frank was right.

I think the entire village was standing around the ramp now. As I opened the door, people were watching anxiously to see who was getting off the airplane. Frank was grinning under his fur lined parka. Everyone seemed very thankful and several volunteered to help unload. Frank took his job as Postmaster seriously. When it came to the U.S. Mail, he stepped forward and took the bright orange bags from my hands. He carefully took the mail from the mailbags and dumped the letters and packages into his leather mail carrier bag. The gathering crowd waited in silence in the below zero cold while he sorted it out. Promptly, he turned to the gathering crowd, began calling names and handing their mail to them. (Under those conditions, it was almost impossible to deliver anything to individual families.)

While this was going on, I handed the bags to my passengers and then groceries and supplies to some anxious folks.

Afterwards, I took one of the passengers aside and quietly asked him how they managed to see the village under those conditions. He grinned and said, "It was easy. You've been following the dog sled trail, all the way from McGrath!"

Although, the folks were mostly Athabascan, 'Eskimo ADF' was a term I came up with for this new resource under the subject of Single Pilot Crew Resource Management. However, to date, I'm the only one who's seemed to have had that experience.

Later on, I found out the winter dog sled trails connected Nikolai to McGrath and networked to other villages. As time went on I found that these folks knew their part of the country extremely well.

Through the course of a few years, I became friends with a lot of the local people out there. Peter Torry, owner of the general store in town, Frank and others became special friends. I received some handmade gifts along the way, a definite honor, which I still have today. Although there are many Russian names, sometimes appearing to be backwards, the village is definitely Native American. Many of the native skills and traditions are still alive there and practiced as daily routine.

During my Wilbur's tour, I had flown into Nikolai a hundred times. Most of the time, routine, if you can call landing on short ice and snow covered gravel strips routine. I'd gotten very good at takeoffs and landings with plenty of room to spare. However, things can happen.

This memorable incident occurred one very cold and snowy day. I had a full aircraft out of Nikolai. My Seneca II with five people and their gear was right at my maximum gross weight. I was heavy, but had calculated takeoff distance for the Seneca II and felt comfortable I could get out with no problem. It had begun to snow heavily and I knew time was of the essence. I had to get out of the area and fast.

After getting everyone aboard, I walked around the aircraft, checking doors and compartments. I got aboard and belted in. The engines started easily and I began my taxi down the runway, carefully keeping the wingtips inside the three foot snow berms lining each side. I was planning to utilize the full length of the runway of course. Best to utilize the full length of any runway, especially a narrow, snow covered bush strip.

Accelerating normally, carefully keeping the wing tips away from the snow berms, I lifted off and began my climb out. Suddenly, "**Bang - Boom**." With the wind noise, I knew a door had popped open! Generally, an open door on a light twin wouldn't cause a problem. This was a back door.

I'd had an incident with an open door on an Aztec a few years back. The airplane when slowed to approach speed became a bucking bronco! You couldn't get the door closed due to horizontal aerodynamic lift. The door was held open six or eight inches or so, creating blanketing of the horizontal stabilator, causing it to stall out at approach speed. I'd also had a stabilator stall in a Seneca over Las Vegas not that long ago. That one was due to icing. In this case, at my present speed, things were stable aerodynamically. However, the wind chill temperature was extremely cold in the cabin. I decided to return to land before all my passengers were frozen and repair or relock the door.

I was somewhat confident about the landing as braking was good on my first one. On short final, I slowed within five knots of my normal approach speed. Things seemed ok. Keeping good pressure on the stabilizer, I hit my normal approach speed at the end of the runway. Easing down between the snow berms now, I flared slightly, floated somewhat, then touched down. Aerodynamic braking – now brakes...nothing. I began to brake off and on with my human antiskid system. Beginning to slow slightly now. However, it was evident I wasn't going to stop in time! The new snow had brought my braking power to practically nil!

I felt there was no choice. I'm taking out a snow berm. I eased the airplane to the right. The wing was clearing the snow bank. 'Not good. Not good. Gotta get my wheels in the snow. More right rudder.' I eased over more, then, my right wheel caught the snow bank. Veering to the right, I began applying left rudder, bringing up the power on the right engine. I was decelerating rapidly now with heavy resistance from the deep snow. Approaching the end of the runway area... 'Hard left rudder now... Right engine...Power up. Power up!' The right engine came alive and began really throwing snow. Suddenly, we popped clear and out of the snow bank. Chopping the power, we came to a stop. I took my time shutting down and sat idling for a time, to see how the engines were running. Things seemed to be okay. I then did a good engine run-up, checked magnetos, listened for any vibrations. Everything seemed okay. This also gave me some time to get over my adrenalin rush and get my heart slowed back to normal.

As I shut the engines down, "Let's check that door."

I followed my right seat passenger out the door and walked around the aircraft with scrutiny. I inspected the aircraft gear, gear doors, props, stabilizer and belly and found no damage and no leaks. Not one antenna had been torn off. On inspection of the door, the upper latch seemed a little worn, but worked ok. I secured the door, made sure everyone was ok to go and strapped in. 'Let's go...One more time'.

None of the passengers had reacted much to the landing and were simply anxious to get going. Through the years of using airplanes as their main transportation, I'm sure they had been through a lot worse. The next takeoff was normal. The flight was routine... Snow, ice, turbulence over the mountains... Just another day.

I was never sure what happened to cause the door to open. Maintenance checked out the aircraft completely, found everything normal.

As I sat in the office, filling out my paperwork for the day, a voice from around the corner,

"Tony, Got a trip for you to Nikolai in the morning. Full boat. Weather might be questionable...Tony! You there?"

I wondered if he felt the draft as I exited out the back door.

CHAPTER 18

RAINY VS PTARMIGAN

A few of you that have read the title of this chapter already know what it's about. You know what I'm going to say about it and already know some of the lessons I'm trying to instill in new guys. Alaska flying is all about making decisions. Making the right choice at the right time comes with experience. Sometimes you have a few hours to plan, sometimes a few minutes, sometimes only a few seconds. There are however, occasional times where the door behind slams shut and you may be totally relying on your skill and experience to stay alive.

Here was yet another day when I was following my friend, Wayne Brockman, flying second section to Fight 501 headed to McGrath, Alaska. The ceiling was 3,000 feet with visibility better than 10 miles. I remained in trail of Wayne as we crossed the Cook Inlet Basin and entered the mountains. We were planning on transitioning the Alaska Range via Rainy Pass, which would get us over in the least amount of time. As we approached the 90 degree turnoff point leading into Rainy Pass, it began to snow.

"Wayne, how's it looking up ahead?" I asked.

"Well, it's not looking real good, light snow, but not looking that bad either," he replied.

"Better take a good look before you go into Rainy," I suggested.

"You're right about that!" he replied.

Both he and I had flown through the pass many times and knew it quite well. The worst part consisted of a couple of good turns around snow covered peaks. That's not bad on a clear day, but it was overcast with a good chance of whiteout should it begin to snow heavier.

"Yeah, Tony, I think I'll take a look. I'll let you know how it is," he said. Wayne made his turn into the pass and a minute later, I was approaching the entrance also. Suddenly, the snow showers picked up in intensity and the pass entrance began to disappear.

I keyed the mike, "Wayne, it's starting to snow pretty hard out here, how's it look?"

"Well, I don't know. It's snowing harder in here also," he answered.

After a brief pause, "Gettin' pretty bad now...Snowing heavier...Gettin' into white out condi..."

"Wayne, say again. You're breaking up. Can you turn around? Wayne..."

At that point, I lost contact with Wayne. I was worried of course as it was snowing very hard now. Visibility had dropped to the point that I could not identify any landmarks looking into the pass entrance.

I took my planned out at this point, banked left and headed down the nice and wide Ptarmigan Pass. Ptarmigan branches off that part of Rainy, goes 25 miles south and then opens out to the west and into the Kuskokwim valley. The feeling is something like you feel turning off a twisting secondary road and jumping on the freeway. We both were low in the mountains and I knew radio reception wasn't that great anyway. However, I had a gnawing feeling going on and continued to attempt contact by every means possible for the next 30 minutes.

As I flew out of Ptarmigan and tundra area, I called Nikolai, the closest village. With no answer, a few minutes later, I radioed McGrath Flight Service and began a communication search for the missing plane. I was feeling quite anxious at this point.

Suddenly I heard a scratchy radio signal, "...Six Juliet Whisky departing Runway... Nikolai..."

I gave him a minute. "Wayne, are you up?"

"Hey, Tony, what's going on?" he said.

"Wayne, how's things? We've been looking for you," I said.

"Sorry 'bout that. Came out of the pass pretty low, went straight over to Nikolai and dropped off the mail. It got pretty tight in the pass there. I always had ground contact, but it sure was snowing. Let's have a coffee in McGrath."

"Sounds great Wayne. How far you out?" I responded.

"Looks like about 11 minutes... see you there." he answered.

As I glanced at my DME, 13 minutes! 'Doggone, he's going to beat me to McGrath...again!'

I was quite relieved of course but concerned at how a seasoned pilot could get into trouble in a couple of minutes in a mountain pass. The answer of course is the forever changing weather. Over coffee, Wayne seemed cool and collected, but after discussion, we both had raised our personal minimums for Rainy Pass.

Mountain passes are dangerous no matter where they are. Alaskan passes are extremely dangerous. I was just glad to have my good friend one more day.

Captain Wayne Brockman and myself ...- cruising home.

CHAPTER 19

SPARRAVOHN AND LIME

Imagine migrating herds of Caribou, thousands, grazing along, brown and beautiful against the blue ponds and lakes, the green meadows and the streaks of white snow. This picture is forever etched in my memory!

Sparravohn LRRS is a USAF early warning radar site with the runway located on the slope of a 3,000 foot mountain. It's hard to imagine all this space age technology sitting in the middle of such a pristine wilderness. The site could only be viewed from above or on short final to the runway.

This 4,000 foot gravel runway follows the slope up. The approach end is close to 1,400 feet elevation. The other end of the runway is close to 1,600 feet. That's more than a 200 foot difference between one end of the runway and the other end!

It's one way in and one way out for takeoff and landing. On short final, you're simply looking at a mountain in front of you. That means of course, you have to land on your first approach. The possibility of a go-around after a bad landing is very slim.

Also, moderate turbulence and wind shear is often encountered when taking off or landing due to the high terrain on all sides. On top of all that, there's a 1,400 foot hill one mile off the end of the approach end of the runway. It took a few times to get the hang of coming in around a mountain on your final approach. You had to practically dive down to the end of the runway, then use 75% power after landing, just to get to the other end where the ramp was located. Landing with a tail wind is not fun at this airport.

After a few landings however, you get to know the terrain a little better and can offset your final approach course approximately 30 degrees which enables you to get down somewhat lower on short final. To accomplish this, it was occasionally necessary to drop down early and proceed around the hill through a ravine which led to the runway.

This is a military airport and is closed to the public, so do not try to get in there without prior permission from the Air Force. The primary structure on the site, other than the runway, appeared, from the air, as a large, white, saucer shaped spacecraft. The additional man-made objects that caught your eye were power stations and antenna arrays. It was a very interesting sight the first time I landed there.

Our men in blue all lived within the main structure which was climate controlled of course. The first time I was invited in to the building, I felt I was entering a space craft. The initial doors opened into a large air lock chamber. From there, you entered into the general lobby and cafeteria area. The living quarters were apartments with doors facing the center space. There were two levels, with most of the apartments upstairs. There was a railing going completely around the border of the upper level, giving the feeling of a sidewalk there. The unit was totally self-contained, with a workout facility, laundry, small store and so on. I didn't manage to get into the radar rooms or any other sensitive military areas. I left with the feeling these guys were indeed living on a ship. It reminded me of my two year tour on a U.S. Navy destroyer.

The airlock is there for a reason. And, if you get locked out for any reason in the dead of winter, you could be dead. Temperatures can drop 50 to 60 degrees below zero, sometimes worse.

A large part of my mission there was to bring groceries and supplies. Usually I was met by the cook who carefully checked off his list for the week.

One such day, I'd landed there under a sunny, bright blue sky. There was no wind. Things seemed great. I opened the door on my Cessna 402 and began to hand out cargo to the guys. I'd handed out about four boxes to Bob Waters, the camp cook, when I suddenly didn't feel my hands.

"Hey Bob, my hands are numb." I mentioned.

"Where's your gloves?" he asked.

"Whoops, forgot. Better get my hands warmed up." I said, as I hurried toward the cockpit.

I grabbed my gloves and began to put them on. This isn't going to work. I couldn't feel my gloves either. I shoved my hands into the back of my ski pants and sat down on them. It felt like sitting on a block of ice. As I sat there, I took a good look at the temperature gauge. Minus 35! I couldn't believe it was minus 35 degrees! Shortly, I regained some feeling and slipped my double gloves on. I learned quickly that clear sunny days can be very deceiving.

Occasionally, there would be times when we couldn't get into the airport due to high winds, low ceilings, or both. Sometimes, when the weather was raging, the mountain would become obscured by clouds lower that the IFR minimums specified on our approach charts.

As the minimums were quite high due to the terrain, if visibility was reported as good below the ceiling, we would fly out to one of the valleys, get down to our lowest vectoring altitude, break out and go in VFR. You really have to know the terrain and have decent visibility below the clouds to accomplish this. The guys at the base sure appreciated us doing that, especially if they had been cut off for days.

On one particularly bad day, I had let down and was proceeding into Sparravohn at low level. As I approached the hill and ravine that advertise the end of the runway, I almost turned around to leave the area. I had eased around the hill with one hand on the throttles careful not to extend beyond my planned out.

'Great'!

The runway came into sight. I eased the throttles back, lowered the nose and selected full flaps.

I knew not to lose the end of the runway at this point, but as I drew closer, the ceiling continued to lower. I was down in the ravine now, watching my wingtips as I slipped through the remaining opening to the runway.

'Whew! Made it.'

As I touched down on the gravel runway, I began to power up so as to make the other end of the runway, or top of the hill so to speak. I liked to keep about 60 knots until close to the end, then ease up on the power and turn into the parking area.

'Wow', I thought. 'That was tight!'

The Force was glad to see me and all the guys were surprised I'd gotten in at all. They'd been isolated for more than a week and were getting low on supplies.

Just about the time I'd finished unloading, I heard a deep rumble. 'What the heck'? We were all mesmerized by a deep throaty sound coming from the ravine.

Suddenly, a brilliant, silver DC-6 appeared at the end of the runway. Now, he's got a wingspan nearly twice mine. 'How'd he do that'?

We watched him land and come rumbling toward us. He hit the top of the hill and turned into the parking area. As he shut down, I closed up my door and drifted over.

As the pilot opened up his door, "Hey, how're you doing?"

"Doin great," I replied. "How bout you?"

"Fine...now. Pretty tight out there!" he said.

"You got that right!" I exclaimed.

I couldn't help but stare at that giant bird sitting on the ramp. Then, I noticed they were unloading barrels of diesel fuel! Calculated risk management is a relative term, I suppose. Later on I found that not only was Northern Air Cargo coming in here with their big birds but also the Air Force was coming in with their C-130 Hercules on occasion! It's all relative I suppose, but also relatively dangerous. I found out later they had previously lost a C-130 on the approach in similar weather with all crew members killed.

Sparravohn and Lime, sounds like some type of Key Lime Pie. Here's the Lime part. The reason I've combined Lime Village with Sparravohn is because they are geographically very close together. Chronologically they were more than a hundred years apart. They were as different as day and night. One is practically on a Star Wars level; the other is a Denaina Athabaskan Indian Village, where most live a sustenance life style. Lime Village was there long before Sparravohn LRRS.

Lime Village is located 160 nautical miles from Anchorage and on the other side of the formidable Alaskan Range. You can imagine the isolation. To get to Lime Village (2AK), as we left Sparravohn, we simply went around to the north side of the mountain and flew 17 miles down to the Stony River. The village lies in a bend in the river somewhat up on a hill. The runway ends are bordered by a north flowing portion and a south flowing portion of the river.

The Sparravohn/Lime Village route involved carrying high ranking military officers, as well as folks going to and from Lime Village. We had a very complex situation most of the time in accomplishing this mission. In addition to Air Force personnel, including officers, we transported mail, local people from the village, kids, dogs, chickens, groceries, cases of pop, snow machine parts and fishing and hunting equipment.

The village runway was short and sandy and varied in length as to level of the river or the amount of precipitation it had received. It was short, with water on both ends. None of the pilots liked going in there as it was somewhat treacherous.

Once again, the village had been isolated for quite some time when I was dispatched on a special charter flight from Anchorage. I was somewhat concerned about the weather conditions. It was spring, with weather moving from the high 20's at night, to the low 40's during the peak of the day. The short runway, I felt could possibly be wet, frozen in places, or both. In other words, Lime Village Airport was in break-up.

No one had been in there for a couple of weeks and my passengers were desperate to get home and to bring in much needed supplies and groceries.

I called ahead and discussed the situation with Randy, the airport manager. After some discussion, it was concluded that the weather and braking action on the runway was good. Visibility was unlimited.

After a quiet, uneventful flight over the mountains, I began my let-down toward my destination. I was heavy with five people, baggage and groceries aboard. However, I knew the limitations of the Seneca II aircraft and knew I was well inside my parameters for this landing. At least I thought I knew.

As I approached, I checked in on the radio. "Lime Village Unicom, Seneca 54JW is approaching 10 miles east - Request advisory."

Randy was standing by, "Winds are calm. Pressure is 30.22.

Captain, your braking action should be good. I just drove my truck down the runway. No problem."

"Okay Randy. Thanks for your help."

As I approached for a closer look, I don't know if I trust that. The runway looks a little shiny, which could possibly mean wet glare ice.

I called again, "Lime Village traffic, Seneca 54JW downwind for runway eight."

"Randy, did you test braking all the way down the runway? Sure looks a little wet, kinda shiny in places."

He came back, "Yes, I did. Braking is good."

"Thanks," as I continued on to left base.

"Seneca 54JW is on left base for runway 10 Lime Village," I called.

Glancing downward momentarily, I noticed the heavy ice flow in the river. As I established my base leg, I lowered flaps to full down position and began slowing to my minimum approach speed.

Now on final, I slowed to the very minimum speed and added a little power to keep from stalling while clipping the bushes at the end of the runway.

Just above stall speed now, I touched down the Seneca II exactly on the end of the 1,500 foot runway.

I held the nose off momentarily, looking for some aerodynamic braking, then gently lowered the nose and raised the manual flaps.

As I touched the brakes however.... we sped up!

I now began braking with rapid, on off brake pedal action. We were not slowing at all. 'This is not good!' I thought to myself!

I considered going around, but I wasn't sure of the condition of the remainder of the runway now. I could see standing water and possibly mud coming up and felt we might not get airborne. I certainly didn't want to go plowing through mud only to end up in the river.

I could see the other end of the runway now. What I was looking at was not a pretty sight. There was no barrier at the end of the runway. From there, the terrain sloped down a 30 foot embankment into the river flowing with ice.

I was still barreling toward the river and went back to full flaps... Got to try aerodynamics again... With full flaps, I lifted the nose off the runway. I wasn't slowing at all. Not good. Not good! The end of the runway and river was coming up fast.

I kicked the rudder full to the right, hoping to get traction in a side slide and maybe some aerodynamic drag from the tail. As

I slipped to the side of the runway, I kicked full left rudder and began my slide to the right. I was slowing somewhat now but it still wasn't enough. I had one more action I could do besides going into the ice jammed river.

A ground loop seemed the best option. I knew it would damage the aircraft but anything was better than going down that river bank.

I kicked full right rudder and began to spin the nose around to the right. As I passed the 90 degree point, the river was all over my windshield!

I added some power to the left engine to continue my spin around. Our momentum toward the river seemed to be subsiding as we went around.

My natural reaction to this new tail slide and to stop the spin-around was to begin powering up the right engine. It was working. It stopped the spin-around action and our momentum toward the river. I felt I was somewhere near the edge of the icy river bank, not fully stopped, but now pointed in the right direction. I continued to push both throttles forward and was at full takeoff power.

That stopped my river-bound tail slide. Now stopped, pointed in the right direction, with engines roaring, we began moving back toward the ramp area!

Within three or four seconds, now moving rapidly toward the ramp, I had to chop both throttles in order to stop and prevent us from hitting the small embankment behind the turn out area. We finally stopped in the turnaround area and were parked where we always parked. I pulled the mixtures back shutting down the engines. All was quiet.

Wow! I thought to myself. Using reverse thrust in a piston aircraft is not something one should try. But, if it keeps you and your folks out of the drink, especially one with icebergs all jammed together and everything, my feeling is do it! It worked that day!

As my passengers deplaned, not a word was said until the last passenger was getting out. She was about 75 I thought.

I steadied her by holding her arm as she stepped out on the ice covered ground. She looked up, caught my eye and in broken English and with an unexcited voice," I didn't think we' za gonna make it."

"Yes Ma'am, it was a little bit slippery but... ahh, no problem!" I replied.

She held out her hand which I took gently and laid my other hand on hers with a warm gesture. She smiled, "Thanks. You can call me Mom now. Everybody else does."

I heard a heavy 'Thud!', 'Clunk!', 'Crack!' and the sound of rushing water. I knew it was the ice flow less than a hundred feet from where we stood.

As she turned and began walking away, I glanced over at the rumbling ice clogged river and let myself go there for a moment. I wondered... if you sink below the ice jammed river surface, how do you get back up through it? That is a tough one.

The last of the baggage and cargo had been unloaded and as I finished closing the doors, I gave Thanks to my Maker, then thanks to my Guardian Angel - again, then charged off to find the airport operations manager. He must have been driving with chains on his tires! He was nowhere to be found.

After thoroughly checking out my muddy aircraft, especially the landing gear, I headed for home.

While we're in still in the vicinity of Sparravohn, as mentioned earlier, there are gigantic herds of Caribou roaming the hillsides. It's a beautiful place to observe these animals as well as other wildlife. I was flying a Piper Turbo Arrow, had dropped off some cargo at Sparravohn and had come out of the mountains at low level. I was thoroughly enjoying observing this massive herd of Caribou, when, at a break in the herd, I noticed a mom and her calf being stalked and very close to being attacked by a huge, brown grizzly. Of course, I took it upon myself to rectify the situation, pulled back on the power and began circling. I slowed down, dropped the landing gear and made a pass at the bear. He looked up, so I had his attention now. I went back around and saw the bear had turned away somewhat. I came at him again, revved the engine this time and got him running. He ran up on a rock outcropping by a small tree and appeared to hang on to it. I circled low and prided myself on breaking up his dinner date.

Suddenly, it hit me.

'What the heck are you doing boy? Do you realize you're low, in a single-engine aircraft, looking a very upset 600 pound grizzly in the eye? What if your engine quits?

Yeah, but I have a gun, a short barrel 12 gauge unplugged pump with .00 buckshot.

Yeah, but what if you're injured, both legs broken and can't get to your gun. Even if you do kill this one, don't you think there are other bears hanging around for these Caribou steak dinners'?

By this time, I had full power up and was gaining altitude. 'Better get on home.'

'I've only got 160 miles to go. Single-engine' I thought, as I began reviewing my survival kit contents. Flight Plan on file, of course, but I knew I could be out there for a few days at best should my engine fail me. Bird shot rounds? You bet. I can hang out for a while if need be. Wow, there's really no civilization between here and Anchorage. I might as well listen to Russian radio through my ADF (low frequency automatic direction finding radio) for a while.

In the wilds of Alaska, if you go down, without an equalizer, you and everyone with you are suddenly very low on the food chain. Even with an equalizer, if you're stranded, it can still quickly become a marginally survivable situation. Not much room for mistakes. Read the materials. Carry the survival gear requirements and more. Attend a survival clinic.

Would you like some more bear stories? You may not want to hear this one.

CHAPTER 20

BEAR MOUNTAIN

'Bear Mountain' is home to one of many Early Warning Radar Sites scattered throughout Alaska. Located in north east Alaska near the Yukon Territory Border, it has one of the most challenging airstrips in the world. Like so many of these sites, they're an oasis' in the wilderness. The reason I was privileged to experience this beautiful area and to have the challenge of landing there was that I transported a maintenance inspector, Bill Carlisle and his gear there to do an inspection and some light repairs.

Now, this airstrip got my attention the day before when I was reviewing the profile on one of the NAV charts –

"Caution: The runway slopes 7.1 % up with a 258 foot differential from one end to the other."

'Ok, the runway is approximately 4,000 feet long, rock and gravel. Obviously, other folks had done it. Must be on the side of another dang mountain and steeper than Sparravohn!'

137

I'll continue this flight for you in a minute, but first, it seems appropriate to tell this story as told by my passenger during the flight. It's a not-so-good bear story.

My passenger's son, Scott, had bought some property just northeast of Anchorage, between Talkeetna and Fairbanks. The property bordered the highway and extended for several acres into the thick forest. He had driven up alone that sunny day with the intention of staking off his property. He found the corner of the property and pulled off onto the shoulder of the road. It was a beautiful, quiet day, blue sky, with very little traffic.

He opened the tailgate, pulled out his single blade razor sharp axe, a bundle of stakes and his high powered rifle. Unable to carry everything, he leaned his loaded rifle up against the truck. His thought was to walk to the edge of the property, then return for his rifle. This was bear country. (All of Alaska is by the way.) He reasoned that he was only going about 50 feet.

He had just dropped the stakes to the ground, when out of the bushes charged a huge grizzly. No time to run. Running's useless anyway against a varmint that can run 40 miles per hour in the thick woods. Scott stood his ground raising his sharp axe to defend himself. The bear lunged forward. Scott swung the axe, hitting him exactly between the eyes, trying to split the bear's skull. As some of you already know, the skull is one of the toughest parts of a bear. Although his head was bleeding profusely, the ferocious bear continued the attack.

Scott was fighting the bear violently with all his might, but suddenly the bear was on top of him, tearing flesh, cracking bones. The bear lifted him up again and again, throwing him to the ground. He was feeling he was going to die and began to lose consciousness. The worst was yet to come. The huge bear moved up to his head, grabbed the entire top of his head in his huge mouth and began to give his kill a death shake. He slung Scott's rag doll body from side to side as if trying to make sure he was dead. Scott was conscious enough to hear his skull cracking and splitting open. When the bear was satisfied the man was dead, he went on about his day.

Sometime later, Greg and Peggy Wilson, a couple from Fairbanks, were driving by. They noticed the gun leaning against the truck with no one around. They had presence of mind enough to pull over and check things out. Looking just off the road, they saw a badly mauled body lying lifeless in the brush. Grabbing their first aid kit, a .44 Caliber Pistol and Scott's loaded rifle, Greg and Peggy cautiously waded through the brush to see if this person was dead or alive.

Laying his fingers on the side of Scott's ankle, Greg felt a weak pulse. That was good news, however, Scott had been terribly mauled, his body was in shreds and half his scalp was torn away. He was alive but was now bleeding profusely from his wounds. They began to put him together the best they could. They used all their first aid bandages but couldn't keep his head together. Greg had the idea of taking off his cap, pressing all the pieces of scalp inside and taping it onto the rest of his head. This act probably saved his life. The ball cap and dressing were actually holding Scott's skull together. After using everything they had for bandages, they together dragged him over to the camper. They pulled him into the back and with Peggy treating his wounds the best she could, sped off to the nearest town and hopefully, a doctor and a clinic.

As of the time of this story, Scott had not recovered fully due to his head and neck injuries. Greg and Peggy Wilson are the reason he survived at all.

There's no major moral to this story, just a small mistake. However, if you wonder why most of the locals, including bush pilots, carry guns, that's why. My preference, mentioned previously, was a 12 gauge Mossberg Pump (unplugged) loaded with .00 buck shot. Some additional advice I've heard, while we're on the subject is that your first shot should be to a front leg or shoulder - try to break him down. Shooting a bear in the head is generally a useless endeavor as the skull is very thick and their head is wedge shaped. A direct hit in the heart may still get you killed by a charging bear. Most of Alaska is still wilderness and yes, when you get off the beaten path, life quickly goes back to basics. Also, without an equalizer and some skill, Hu becomes a creature quite far down the food chain.

Now I know it's hard to understand if you are from LA, love animals and think that all bears are fuzzy and cuddly, but here's the advice. If you go outside the city limits of Anchorage, you better have a gun aboard, not a pea shooter, a real gun! My heart goes out to Bill, Scott and their family. I am in great hopes that things are going well for them.

An interesting thing about grizzlies and brown bears, I am told, is that they don't like the taste of humans. Play dead with these creatures, but fight a black bear to the death. Black bears do like you and they'll have you for dinner. There's a possibility this bear had a moose kill in the area, however, neither the bear nor any other animal remains were found.

If you would like to weigh in the power of a huge grizzly, here's another tidbit. Grizzly bears have been known to rip black bears to shreds when crossing paths. The grizzly will eat a black bear for dinner and have been known to dig them out of their dens.

Of course, a black bear is nothing to play with either. If you climbed a 50 foot tree, he'd be right behind you.

While traveling on a back road near Seward, I surprised a good sized one. He was startled it seems and took off at a full gallop, hit the base of a 90 foot tree and didn't slow his pace up until approximately 40 feet in the air. He hung there like a squirrel and looked back at me. I was totally amazed and slowly moved on.

When bears are getting hungry, they don't leave a post-it note, they shred trees, turn over logs and flip rocks around. Always look for the signs. Make noise.

Now, let's continue to "Bear Mountain," which is actually Indian Mountain by name. We occasionally flew inspectors, machines, personnel and supplies into this remote outpost. The site is similar to Sparravohn, primarily because many were built with the same technology and by the same contractors. This one, however, is even more remote and hidden in the surrounding mountains. When you arrive overhead, it appears from the air that a UFO (a large disk shaped object) had landed at the base of this steep mountain. Actually the large white domes and various antenna arrays are much the same as Sparravohn's.

The first landing and takeoff I made there was very exciting of course. At first glance, it was "No Way Hosea!!!" However, after some analysis, good planning and proper attention to my instruments, I realized it could be done.

That particular day, I began calling 20 miles out. I had a planned arrival time with the Air Force and arrived at the approximate planned time. After calling every three or four miles inbound on the published frequencies and others, I decided to over-fly the dome and try to get someone's attention. "Indian Mountain, Indian Mountain, this is 4323Q overhead now, requesting advisory. EARLY WARNING RADAR SITE!! HELLO!!"

After buzzing the tower so to speak, with no response, I decided to land.

The landing approach involved a descent into a narrow valley between two steep mountain slopes, then a 90 degree left turn onto a very short final. It was a tight approach and I had the feeling of having to fly into a hole, not onto a mountain!

I dropped into a small canyon on my base leg, well below the surrounding terrain. At this point, I was committed to my landing. There were no other choices besides plowing into the mountainside. My view was nothing but terrain now, terrain as in mountain slopes of all different angles. After a slight turn in the canyon, the alien spacecraft appeared directly ahead. I was surprised to see we were at about the same elevation. Within a few seconds, I began my fairly steep left turn onto a very short final approach. As my right wing passed beside the large futuristic metallic dome, "I did everything except blow the horn and yell, Hi Y'all!"

On short final, I wasn't really focused on anything except the runway and my instruments of course. The facility became simply a blur under my right wing.

The reason for watching your gauges closely is that your perceptions are not necessarily reality. The angle to the runway is extremely steep. Forget the full stall landing. You seem to land in a climb attitude. The landing was interesting as I felt like a fly lighting on the wall where I basically kept flying the airplane until my wheels were rolling in the rocks. I don't know what the vertical speed indicator was showing at the touchdown point, but shortly thereafter we were in a climb! There was no time to look at gauges at that point. You simply keep your speed up, your power up and make sure you're using good judgment in your climb to the top the hill.

It's a power landing and a power taxi. If you reduce power too much, the aircraft will tend to stop. This definitely is not a good thing on a steep, uphill, soft, dirt runway with one and two inch rocks. You have to keep the power up until you crest the top of the hill. That is the end of the runway. Cresting the hill is a maneuver itself. When that occurs, you have to chop the power and make an immediate right turn onto the ramp area. There's not much room for error.

That day, after all the calls, two flybys and a power on landing on their runway, still, no one showed up. Normally they were there waiting for us at the ramp in their 4X4. Well, after waiting 20 minutes, we decided to hike down the runway which meant down the mountain. That turned out to be a pretty good walk of almost a mile. I felt quite uncomfortable leaving my weapon in the airplane but knew I would feel even more uncomfortable, brandishing a shotgun and surprising a bunch of isolated military guys.

We finally got to the door of the futuristic structure. The air lock door was open, so we walked right in. We sat down our gear and walked into the mess hall (cafeteria). We were standing around, spotted some coffee and were about to have a cup, when one of the guys walked in. He stood there for a moment and looked at us with a quizzical look. "WHO THE HECK ARE YOU?"

By this time three other pretty uptight troops arrived. We were explaining as fast as we could, when suddenly, a clipboard appeared in front of my face. "Here. Fill this out."

After that was over, the realization had fully set in that an aircraft had repeatedly tried to be seen and heard, had landed and the occupants had walked into their establishment unseen. Needless to say, we were treated very well after that.

Bill announced, "Well boys, I've got to get to work. Gotta get out of here before nightfall."

I agreed and mentioned, "If you need any help from me Bill, just let me know."

As I was still edgy from the gruesome bear story, a spectacular landing in space, walking a mile or so unarmed in bear country and walking unannounced into a secure military site, being in trouble, believe me, I was very relieved to simply kick back, watch a little TV and spend some time in the mess hall.

After a time, the cook began to prepare lunch for the crew. I could hear pots and pans rattling around and began to smell the aroma of tomato soup cooking. Eventually, he stuck his head out the door and said, "Hey, how're you doing? Care to sample some soup?"

'I could definitely use some soul food' "You bet. Thanks."

He sat the soup on the counter and kept working away.

At one point, he decided to take a break and wandered out with a cup of coffee. He asked some things about the flight and remarked how interesting it was that we'd been completely missed by everyone at an early warning radar site. I agreed.

The subject of bears came up. He was appalled at the story I repeated to him about Bill's son. As it turned out, he had a few bear stories of his own.

"Some of the guys like to hunt and fish for recreation and have bear encounters all the time. You better believe, none of us go anywhere without our weapons."

He continued, "Just Saturday, we were in the middle of dinner, when out of the corner of my eye, I caught a large black image just inside the door. No one moved."

"It was warm that day, the main doors and the inner doors had been left open."

This huge black bear walked right in and continued to wander past the 12 men eating dinner and didn't even look at them. The men were frozen. He continued out of the mess hall and wandered down one of the hallways. He turned and entered one of the open sleeping quarters, looked around momentarily, proceeded to the windowsill and took a shiny red apple someone had sat there to ripen. While chomping on the apple, he reentered the mess hall, spotted the door and went out.

The cook confessed, he thought about picking up a broom and shooing it out, but decided not to disturb the situation - Strange but true.

Well, Bill came up and had completed his work. The guys were great, showed us around some more. Then, after a great lunch, we were in a 4X4 headed up the hill to our aircraft.

The departure was even more interesting than the landing. We got aboard, closed the door and started the engine. The feeling was somewhat like my first solo flight. You're going to do it. You think you know what's going to happen and hope your training pays off!

Well, after thoroughly reviewing the checklist and completing a complete engine run-up, I eased toward the edge of the ramp.

"You ready for this?" I asked my wide eyed passenger?

"You bet. Let's go home." He replied.

I glanced at his seat belt and gave it a tug. There we were, perched on the crest of what looked like a ski jump in the Winter Olympics.

I set flaps at 25 degrees for the shortest ground roll. Then, it was over the top, pointing straight down the slope now. More power, 40, 50, 60 knots. It was a little bouncy in the rocks, 70 knots, back pressure now. 'You're still at 10 degrees nose down! Keep an eye on the gauges' (Instruments) I tell myself, as the aircraft simply moved away from the steep mountainside. The feeling is more of a vertical lift off of a helicopter.

With the steep mountains surrounding us and with a nose down attitude, the initial feeling was disorientation, almost vertigo. I definitely watched the gauges right after liftoff. As my airspeed increased rapidly, I smoothly pulled the nose up to compensate, quickly lost site of the runway environment, began a right turn and placed the alien space craft in my six. Soon I was maneuvering through the narrow mountain passes, headed back toward Anchorage.

If you ever get a chance to take the Bear Mountain Challenge, remember, your perceptions will be distorted on landing and on takeoff. I strongly recommend you keep an eye on the gauges until you are sure the earth and sky are in their proper places.

Although most of the radar sites in Alaska are exciting as well as challenging, this one had to beat them all. Yes, landing there would be a challenge for any pilot. But again, don't go there unless you have business there. Those guys are armed. Prior permission is required by the Air Force! You might find yourself under arrest or worse, stuck in a remote area without an airplane.

Also, after our little fly in episode, they seemed to tighten up their security measures.

You must remember, this was long before the infamous 9/11 attack on the U.S. I'm sure things are a lot different these days. There's a good reason these LRRS (Long Range Radar Sites) exist. Let's talk about bears of a different type.

CHAPTER 21

BEARS OF A DIFFERENT SORT

Galena, Alaska airport ... 'Looks normal enough, but, what's up with the arrestor cables on both ends of the runway?'

Located in the middle of Alaska, this quiet looking place was home to several military fighter aircraft. It's a joint military and civilian airport and is in a good position to be an Air Force Soviet Bomber interceptor base. This airport has been used repeatedly as a U.S. Forest Service fire fighting base as well.

During fire season, I delivered Smoke Jumpers and their gear to various locations around Alaska. These guys were extremely courageous, well-disciplined and physically fit. I believe that many are ex-military looking for a fire fight of a different kind. These brave firefighters parachute into the toughest, hottest, trouble areas.

I'd dropped a fire crew off in Galena, which appeared that day to be a war time staging area. In a way, that's exactly what it was. As I was refueling that day, I caught some of the line guys eating lunch, where, in our general conversation, I brought up the early warning radar site event. This brought up a discussion about

149

Alaska's close proximity to Russia and the on-going military activity. One of the guys brought up an unbelievable story. Funny, I don't remember reading about it in the Anchorage Daily News or seeing it on the Today Show.

The guys were out on the ramp fueling aircraft as usual. There was a sudden thundering jet noise. They looked up and saw a jet in slow flight, with gear and flaps extended, apparently making a landing. As the aircraft approached the end of the runway, it began to power up and apparently was planning a go around. As it approached the tower area, suddenly they saw the big red star on the tail. Remember, this was long before the end of the Cold War.

As the craft passed by, they could all see the pilot flipping off the tower! The Russian Mig broke off to the right, then made a nice 270 degree left turn back to the opposite runway. By this time, the military was severely scrambling to launch. As the Mig approached the tower for the second time, he flipped them off again, pulled up his landing gear and went to full afterburner. In less than 10 seconds, he had disappeared over the horizon. By the time the first F16 taxied to the end of the runway, the Mig was deep inside Russia. The pilot, I suppose, had delivered a coup to the Americans!

This was prior to the upgrade of the Early Warning Radar System. About a year later, I heard the Air Force was testing a new over the horizon radar to help them see low level aircraft.

Alaska's proximity to Russia has caused a multitude of problems for the military. Even after the Cold War supposedly ended, there was still probing going on by Russia. In one month, there had been 41 Bear Bomber intercept events occurring all along the borders. I'm sure these cat and mouse games still go on in the air and in the sea. A strong vigilance by our military is a wonderful thing.

As a resident in Anchorage during the cold war, along with earthquakes, volcanoes and tsunamis, you were happy to know you had a whole eight minutes to prepare for a Soviet nuclear missile attack. You could just about make it to the nearest grocery store, run in and lock yourself in the freezer. At least your remains would be preserved. Things are quite a bit better in today's world.

Returning from a med-evac mission on a beautiful clear day, I was able to witness an intercept. It was quite a spectacular site. We were in a Cessna Conquest II at 27,000 feet headed toward Anchorage, traveling along the northwest coast. We were somewhere just south of Nome. The military traffic was given to us by center as they approached our altitude. They went by us at extremely high speed in what looked like near vertical flight. The two F-16's in formation separated just after passing us and moved off in opposite directions. However, shortly, they began a converging maneuver. Studying their point of convergence, we saw a silvery glint. Then the Bear Bomber came into view. Seconds later, a third F-16 came rocketing by us, also going to the party. As they all converged, we observed a slow 180 degree turn back to the west.

We just sat there with our mouths open. Let's see. We were headed south on the west coast, toward Anchorage. This event occurred mostly in our ten o'clock high position. That would mean, they were deep over Alaska!

There are some real interesting pictures hanging around Elmendorf Air Force base for you non-believers. Although I've been away for a while, I would bet you a box of doughnuts this still goes on.

A good friend of mine, a Native American lady, was born and raised in Wales, Alaska. It's a small village north of Nome and very close to the Russian coast. We were discussing one day, the "Wall coming down and the normalization of relations with Russia." She was born and raised only a few miles from the border. "Normalization?" she said in her Alaskan dialect. "Half my relatives live in Russia. We've been visiting each other as long as I can remember." Being in her 40's at the time, I believe that was long before the 'Wall came down.' In the winter, the narrow ocean in the Diomede Island area freezes solid allowing sled dogs and snow machines to travel back and forth. Every year they had a carnival with trading booths and were generally over-run by Russian relatives.

The Russian influence is seen everywhere. Almost every village of any size has a Russian Orthodox Church. In and around the Churches and cemeteries you can see an interesting mix of Russian and Native American Icons and symbols displayed.

One of the companies I worked for, Rocky Mountain Helicopters, I believe, was very effective in helping to tear down the Cold War barriers. They, along with Providence Hospital and the University of Alaska, had tried for some time to get permission to provide air ambulance services to some of the coastal Russian cities closest to Anchorage. I'll have more on this later in a later chapter - World Impact.

One of the great things I liked about flying in Alaska was the diversity of flight duties, the challenges, the people and the totally awesome geographical extremes.

Let's leave the mountains of the Alaska Range and the interior and head down south to the most pristine water wilderness in the world. It can be as deadly as it is beautiful.

CHAPTER 22

FLYING THE SOUND

It takes a special kind of person to be a pilot in Alaska. You've got to be part adventurer, part explorer and tough as nails when it comes to piloting. You did have to be tough enough so to speak, to get by Joe and Rich Wilbur of 'Wilbur's, the Family Airline'.

Wilbur's pilots had to be physically and mentally strong and able to handle a situation while remaining cool under pressure. However, toughness didn't necessarily mean you would pass the grade. You had to demonstrate the skills, think on your feet and be very knowledgeable in your profession.

Due to the severe terrain mixed with unpredictable weather, heavy, intense training was the standard and was a big issue with them. If you were signed off by Rich Wilbur to fly into Valdez or any of our other destinations, you had the knowledge and skills to stay alive out there, no matter what the situation. Rich had an uncanny, magical touch with an airplane and was a tremendous instructor and check pilot. Other Wilbur's pilots were well trained, knew the challenging terrain and could read the situation they were in, or were about to encounter. Adding that to Wilbur's special flight procedures (generally approved by the F.A.A.) enabled us to safely negotiate through seemingly impossible odds. Some procedures were company specific (no other company had them). Each Wilbur's pilot had to take a flight check, proving they could accurately fly the procedures before they were assigned the route. As time went on, I came to really appreciate the vigorous training we'd received.

Nowhere in Alaska, was the heavy training regimen more important than within the Prince William Sound area. Our passengers generally had no idea of the training that went into developing a confident, skilled pilot who generally made their flights go smoothly.

For example, one late spring day, on a flight into Valdez, Alaska, a passenger tapped me on the shoulder and said, "Captain Tony, you've got a job everybody wants but nobody has! This is just about the most beautiful place I have ever seen!"

"Yes, it is beautiful today." I replied.

We'd just broken out of the clouds at 5,000 feet about to pass over the Valdez Narrows, looking ahead at the beautiful, water-filled canyons of the Valdez Arm. It was nice and clear ahead, as is often the case. In the distance, you could make out the city of Valdez, pronounced Valdeeze, standing white between the shoreline and snowcapped mountains.

I definitely agreed with my passenger, but held my reserve about his first statement. Today, the air was calm over the Prince William Sound, so smooth you had the feeling of sitting on your living room sofa and looking out a picture window... 'If he had been aboard three days ago'. Springtime snow and ice can and generally does cause radical problems for airplanes.

The route from Anchorage to Valdez was absolutely beautiful. If the weather was good, we'd fly up the Turnagain Arm, just south of Anchorage, through the Portage Pass, over the seaport town of Whittier, by Esther Island, Glacier Island and as winds and weather permitted, would continue across the face of the mighty Columbia Glacier.

This glacier is both beautiful and majestic. It's white, icy face rises dramatically from the blue water. Constantly calving, the glacier litters the adjacent ocean with icebergs of all sizes creating favorite sunning places for the numerous seals and birds.

The Columbia Glacier covers an area larger than the state of Rhode Island. This river of ice and snow winds out of site up into towering snow covered mountains and extends to the edge of the water. On occasion, I've been lucky enough to catch site of calving and watched large sections of the glacier break away and crash spectacularly into the water. The wave action is tremendous, but doesn't seem to bother the various seals and sea lions basking in the sun on their bobbing icebergs.

On this route, we'd pass just north of the soon to be infamous Bligh Island, through the Valdez Narrows and into the Port of Valdez.

Bligh Island... Let's get some perspective. Prior to the Exxon Valdez running aground on this magnificent island, we generally had to fly higher or increase our distance from the island due to the millions of beautiful birds. When they flew, the entire horizon would become blanketed with white, looking like a large white curtain shifting with the winds. The day after, only a few were seen. Three days later, there was not one bird in the air. There's more of this story later on.

I loved taking this route if the weather was decent but hated it when the Sound was kicking up.

I reminded my passengers to make sure their belts were fastened, then I took a moment in time, took a deep breath and let my surroundings absorb into my soul. 'He's right; it is the most beautiful place on earth'. I glanced at the sparkling white Columbia Glacier just off to my left, its vertical ice cliffs reflecting in the bluest blue water below. Ahead were the Narrows, with solid rock walls rising on both sides of the narrow water canyon, their peaks cutting into the deep blue sky, their bases diving into the crystal clear deep waters.

When you pass through the Narrows, you break out into the beautiful green Valdez Valley surrounded by snow-capped pyramid-shaped mountains with bright white glaciers spilling into the water. The ice cold glaciated ocean water below you is now more green than blue and reflects the entire scene. The mountains tower above you both left and right, rising vertically out of the valley and shooting up into the sky. As you approach Valdez, one particularly ominous mountain of rock rises more than 7,000 feet right behind the city. The much higher snowcapped mountains in the area rise over 14,000 feet and give the impression you're in Switzerland. Valdez, often referred to as 'Little Switzerland', is almost completely surrounded by these majestic pyramid shaped mountains. However, I think it's even more dramatic in that it's located on this pristine and glaciated deep water port. To give you some perspective, the tallest peaks of the Rocky Mountains near Denver, Colorado have roughly a 9,000 foot vertical rise from the area elevation. In contrast, these mountains rise dramatically out of the sea to over 14,000 feet.

As you approach the city, you'll occasionally pass over cruise ships, huge oil tankers and fishing boats coming in or leaving the busy sea port. You may ask, what are the supertankers doing here? Well, Valdez happens to be the termination point of the Alaska Oil Pipeline.

The 800 mile pipeline connects Prudoe Bay to the Valdez terminal and is capable of delivering 2,000,000 barrels of crude oil every day.

Let's get back in our airplane.

Generally, if you are flying this route, it's recommended you call on air to air frequency approaching any of the popular scenic tour attractions. We always reported approaching the Columbia Glacier, entering the Narrows, leaving the Narrows and approaching the airport area.

I did meet a No-Rad Aero Commander, head on, down on the face of the glacier once. No-Rad's a term for no radio, not talking. He was on the inside, meaning closer to the face of the glacier. I veered right to avoid a collision and I'm not sure if he ever saw me. Pilots, remember, scenery is for your passengers. Stay vigilant.

We approached the airport with only a few minor bumps, had a nice landing and taxied toward the terminal building. The Cessna 402's setup required that the pilot exit the aircraft first, followed by the passengers. That enabled us to take good care of our door, monitor and assist passengers coming down the steps. Occasionally, the ramp agent would meet us and assist. Generally, people were excited and thankful for a good flight.

After my passengers had left the aircraft for the terminal this particular day, I was walking around the airplane and stopped to glance up at the mountainside to the North. Suddenly there was

159

a rumble and as I watched, a formidable land slide took place. First dust was visible, appearing as smoke on the mountainside. Then rocks began to move, sliding down toward the unsuspecting water. As the avalanche moved, it continued to gain speed until it was dropping with tremendous force. Crashing into the water, it created a large wave moving toward the opposite shoreline. The incident was quickly over as the wave slowly settled into the surface. Only a few two foot waves hit our side of the bay. - Just another day at the office.

Valdez is the land of tremors, landslides and tsunamis.

The Valdez of today is the new town. Old Valdez, or the remains of it, lies just to the south. There's not much there following the 1964 earthquake and tsunami which followed. It seems this beautiful bay one day suddenly lost all of its water. Shortly after this wonderment, a hundred foot wall of water reentered the valley through the Narrows and destroyed everything in its path. Many were killed by this terrifying event. There's actually some footage of the event at the downtown Earthquake Museum in Anchorage.

The new Valdez is a small but fairly modern town with all the amenities we're used to. It also has a large fish hatchery where they release Salmon on occasion. It's interesting to watch the salmon attempting to reenter the hatchery building during spawning season. They're literally jumping up and hitting the side of the building. Fishing is really great and wildlife is abundant around both towns and throughout the Sound.

Flight 301, depending on weather of course, ran daily, twice a day. Occasionally, seats would be available where company personnel and families could jump seat down just to spend the day or go fishing. One such day, I was privileged to take my family down to Valdez to enjoy the sights and do a little fishing. After spending some time around town, we picked up our fishing gear and headed to a recommended spot just south of town.

Jennifer, my 10 year old daughter, caught her first fish that day, a 15 pound Silver salmon. She's pretty independent and insisted on wrestling that fish for 25 minutes! She finally won and we and the neighbors had good eats for a week!

Later the same day, we were on a hike along one of many interesting trails near Valdez when my son, Paul, also caught a fish. He didn't use fishing gear, but ambushed a huge salmon in a stream, caught it by the tail,

"Hey, Dad, I caught a big one!" I looked around at the sight. That fish was more than half his size, writhing back and forth trying to get loose.

For such an amazing feat, I was very proud of him, but...I hated to break the news to him.

"Paul, you've got to put it back. It's illegal to grab fish out of the streams."

"Well, bears do it!"

After a short argument, he let the fish go and was quite depressed for the rest of the day. It's got to be a memorable experience for both kids!

CHAPTER 23

VISITING SEAPORTS ON THE SOUND

Valdez, Cordova and Whittier are the most populated towns on the coast of the Prince William Sound. The Sound is a large body of water dotted with islands and pristine harbors, generally accessible by float plane or boat only. The water is generally pretty cold with occasional trains of icebergs drifting with the currents. Other settlements are scattered and small. Some consist of only one or two buildings. The Sound, although quite cold, is home to many types of sea life, from Seals to Killer Whales.

On occasion, our daily Anchorage to Valdez route would continue on to the beautiful town of Cordova. After takeoff from Valdez, we'd head southwest back through the Narrows, then head south along the coast by the village of Tatitlek. From there, we flew over Hawkins Island, then over the town, through a gap in the mountains, over the marina and land at this great airport.

Cordova is a picturesque seaport town accessible only by plane or boat. In general it appears a little more rustic than Valdez. There are absolutely no roads to Cordova. That's one thing that makes it very unique and in effect, an island community. It also was affected by the 1964 earthquake. The floor of the sound in the area was lifted approximately 10 feet and created the mud flats adjacent to the town.

Cordova is lush with vegetation in the summer and has a large population of bears and other wildlife. I loved the people in both towns and enjoyed spending time there when I could. Some of the best Silver Salmon fishing in the world lies just around the corner from Cordova.

I've checked out most of the islands from time to time and I actually had the opportunity to land on Hinchinbrook Island at Johnston Point and deliver some parts for the VOR there. VOR stands for Very High Frequency Omni-Directional Range and is a navigational aid for airmen. The runway is 1,700 feet, sand, but not bad. The Cessna 206 had no trouble negotiating the strip. It is government owned and private, so don't land there without permission.

Some other memorable sights there have been bears, bears doing what bears do and occasionally observing bears swimming from one island to the next.

Pods of humpbacks and other types of whale are easily observed in the crystal clear waters from above. It's easy. You just catch a whale breaching and drift over in that direction. It's best to stay at least 1,500 feet or so to keep from harassing the animals.

Killer Whales, actually an over-grown porpoise species, are easily spotted from the air also. Sometimes Dall's Porpoise are confused with Killer Whales because of the color. The quickest way to tell the difference is that the Killer Whale has a tall dorsal fin.

Dall's Porpoise roam the crystal clear waters of the Prince William Sound

Among the tremendous variety of birds is everything from the small Puffin to large Bald Eagles. Native American Legend has it that there are 'Thunder Birds' that roam the remote skies in some parts of Alaska. Actually, I've talked to people who swear they've observed these huge birds with 25 foot wingspan. Sea Otters and all kinds of other varmints are abundant.

Most of all, flying low across the sound has to take the first prize for all my flying in Alaska. To weave in and out of the fiords and around the islands at low level, is an unbelievable experience. Being in a multi-engine aircraft or float plane gives you a little more feeling of comfort simply because there's no landing spots should you lose your engine. There's lots of rocks and water with very few beaches. The islands themselves are generally steep and rugged, great for birds, but that's about it.

Not many suitable beaches for landing around here!

CHAPTER 24

CORK IN THE WATER

Don Adams, a pilot friend of mine, thought he was safe and secure in his Cessna 185 on floats while flying back and forth across the Sound from Cordova. This is his story.

It was late as he traveled across the ocean below him. Suddenly, he heard the engine misfire. A few seconds later – silence.

The first thing he felt, as we all do, is disbelief. This can't be happening. Then, "Best Glide Speed... Gas, Mixtures, Boost Pump, Checklist" he shouted, becoming his own best copilot... "Got plenty of gas... Must be the fuel pump."

"Best landing spot and turn to it. Well! I'm over an entire ocean! I've got floats! Attempt to restart!" Out of 1,500 feet now and he couldn't get the engine to even cough. He fumbled under the seat, grabbing his life jacket.

"Better put this on!" Changing hands on the yoke he got one arm in at a time, strapping on his life jacket. He cinched it up tight.

"Land parallel to the swells." As he negotiated the aircraft to line up perfectly, knowing he must be right on speed in case the

167

swell suddenly dropped out from under him. Too slow, could mean a stall, nosing him in, breaking the windshield and the airplane badly and more than likely injuring his body.

At 20 feet he could hear his heart pounding. Now with a little more crosswind he had to lower the left wing apparently below the crest of the oncoming wave.

"Attitude! Attitude! Attitude!" His left float touched the water.

"Keep flying!" The other float touched. The front of the floats plowed into the water.

"Back pressure!"

The airplane decelerated rapidly with a sinking motion. Straining on the wheel he wasn't sure if he was accomplishing anything. Suddenly the floats popped up. He hadn't flipped over. He did things right making a very tricky dead stick landing in some moderate swells.

"Thank You, Jesus!"

As the airplane came to a stop, he continued to give thanks breathing several strong sighs of relief. He then began his shutdown checklist.

His victory was short lived, however. In less than three minutes, he had become a cork floating in the ocean. As the sun settled below the mountains, the realization that he might be there a while slowly sank in. No one's coming out here after dark!

Hoping the swells wouldn't get any worse, he made his last radio call and climbed into the back seat to try to get some sleep. About the time he closed his eyes, something large bumped into his floats from the right side causing him to press against the side of the cabin. Grabbing his flashlight, he shot the beam out the right window. The float looked okay. As he glanced a little farther out into the now black water, he saw some movement. A very large fin was slowly submerging. That was just a little too close. This was the story throughout the night as he had to spend the night bobbing around in a black ocean. Large hungry things kept bumping into his floats, checking him out all night, a very long, cold, lonesome and uneasy night.

As day began to break, he turned on the radio. He made a few more calls on various frequencies and nothing...when suddenly; "72Z, this is 53Q...You on?" came a cheerful voice.

"You betcha! Who's this?" Don replied.

"This is John. I've got David, tools and some parts. Boat from Tatitlek is just about to you. I've got you in sight. See you in a minute."

"'Bout time you guys got here. I'm tired of being fish bait!" he retorted.

53Q appeared overhead circling to the left for a landing. As they began their descent to land, the aircraft disappeared momentarily. He could still hear the engine over the sounds of the ocean although he had lost sight of them. The swells were lighter but still somewhat of problem. Eventually, they came taxiing up, shutting down 30 feet away. They were both out on the floats at this point.

"Boat'll be here in a few minutes. We won't get too close. Don't need two broken aircraft out here." John shouted.

"Got any breakfast?" Don shouted.

"How about some good hot coffee, Caribou Sausage, Eggs and Biscuits?" David called out from inside the rescue plane.

"Man, that sounds plumb wonderful," Don shouted back with enthusiasm.

"Well, we ain't got nothing. Couldn't get it to you anyway," David shouted. The guys laughed.

"Very Funny!" Don shouted.

"I believe they've got some breakfast for you on the boat." John shouted.

As the drone of the boat began to penetrate the sounds of the ocean, Don contemplated what a wakeup call it had been, to go from feeling like a king, to becoming another link in the food chain. And, to have comrades like these that would come out to the middle of the sound and help him out. That's just awesome.

The rescue boat was a fishing boat from Tatitlek, the crew had heard the May Day call and responded at the break of day. As they approached, the Native American crew dropped their runabout into the water and began shuttling tools and people between the floating aircraft.

Don knew his guys were good and that he would be up and going soon. Just after he'd finished a good breakfast and his second cup of coffee, he was.

CHAPTER 25

CIRCLES IN THE WATER

On a return flight from Cordova to Anchorage one beautiful day, cruising VFR, (visual flight rules) at about 2,000 feet, I spotted a perfectly symmetrical circle in the water. Flying alone I dropped down to see what was causing it. From the perfect circle my immediate impression was that it was a mechanical man made, propeller driven device gone wild. As I got lower, I began to see two objects one behind the other. When right over the scene I banked hard left and couldn't believe my eyes. There was a large killer whale chomping at the tail of a large seal simply trying to out-maneuver the much larger animal. The seal was practically airborne most of the time. The whale was relentless in the tightest turn he could manage. I don't know how it came out as I had to get back to Anchorage.

My other circle in the water story occurs on a day when enroute from Valdez to Cordova. I had just left the Valdez Narrows, when the rain began. I was only able to climb to 2,000 feet, remaining below the ceiling. I was receiving the nav aid signal from Johnston Point V.O.R. and decided to proceed in that direction away from the mountains. Suddenly, the weather worsened. There was no one to talk to below 3,000 feet in the area. I knew I definitely needed to get out of this as soon as possible.

The rain began pounding heavier on the windshield, drowning out the engine noise. After a couple of minutes, I was considering a 180 to get back to Valdez when I noticed the sunlight ahead.

I said to my invisible Co-Pilot, "Getting lighter ahead." 'That's very good'. Seeing the lightening clouds and streams of sunlight ahead, I knew I would soon be out of the rain. 'Getting brighter now, Yes!'

The rain let up and suddenly I was out in the open.

I had just reached for my sunglasses, when... 'Doesn't look right... Perfectly curved wall of rain on my right.' Something caught my attention to my left.

"Dang! Water Spout!" Another perfect circle in the water, with a major tower of water spiraling skyward from the surface. I went into a steep turn, 90 degrees to my flight path and penetrated the solid wall of gray and the heavy rain ahead.

I continued to move away from the scene, sweating bullets again, raining inside and outside. I gradually began a slow turn back toward Johnston Point. Finally, I began to break out and was soon out of the low clouds and the rain completely.

Looking back, I could see the tremendous tops of the thunderstorms I was leaving. Thunderstorms were practically unheard of in Alaska at the time. Now, I hear they're more common. When I first arrived in Alaska, I was told thunderstorms would never be a problem here.

"Don't ever say 'never', especially in Alaska."

Now I'm told the weather is changing for sure as the average temperature last year was three degrees higher than normal. That's bound to change some weather patterns and terrain as well.

CHAPTER 26

THE SOUND IN WINTER

OK, so much for the good old days of summer. Let's talk about some winter flying over the Prince William Sound. Winter and night occurs for all practical purposes around October and ends about April. Ask a local when fall occurs. A possible answer would be "On Tuesday. All the leaves freeze and fall off!" It is a short period for sure.

Around these latitudes, it gets light around ten in the morning and begins getting dark around three in the afternoon. So, when your flights are at seven in the morning and five in the evening, it's always dark. Add wicked winds, snow and icing conditions, to the darkness and you get a real interesting gumbo of problems.

One month in December I believe I set my personal record for logging more night IFR than VFR. For 32 flights straight, the only outside reference I had was the runway lights at Anchorage and the runway lights at Valdez and Cordova. Flying on instruments all the time combined with turbulence and icing conditions at night created a somewhat surrealistic environment.

We were flying non-pressurized equipment so we were always in the weather. That particular season, the City of Valdez was no longer measuring snow in inches but in feet. It seems we had 86 feet of snow in Valdez that season and generally whatever falls, stays until spring. There was virtually a snow mountain created by bulldozers and plows that was higher than the tallest building at the airport.

Conditions change rapidly in both Valdez and Cordova and after a couple of missed approaches in the ice and fog over Valdez, with rocks on all sides and living to tell about it, I raised my personal minimums. In other words, I gave myself an extra thousand feet of ceiling before I would even consider launching from Anchorage. There have been many crashes into the rocks around Valdez, including accidents involving sophisticated military aircraft with well-trained crews. Due to the danger of mixing weather and terrain, the route to Valdez is littered with hundreds of crashed airplanes, especially in the Portage Pass area above Whittier.

To offset this inherent danger, we made a practice of going through the narrows on good days at low level. We learned all the landmarks between the narrows and the Valdez airport. Why? Because even though the weather was reportedly good in the narrows and good at the airport, occasionally fog would build in-between. We also had the localizer tuned in as we rounded the narrows just in case we hit a fog bank. There was no turning around in the narrows! And, if this were to happen, we had developed an escape plan. We set up the localizer as we entered the narrows, then simply tracked the localizer to the runway. We experimented in VFR conditions and found that it could work in a low level emergency. One of our guys had this happen to him as he entered the narrows. It was VFR at the airport, but he suddenly was trapped in fog between the vertical rock walls. He actually used our escape route and landed with no problems.

About the only thing scarier than an instrument approach near rocks over water is a missed approach.

The LDA DME-C was the name of the localizer approach into the Valdez valley. It's the quickest approach in and safe as long as you stay within the limitations indicated. Even though you "fly the numbers" it can still quickly become a somewhat hairy approach at times. This is especially true on the route from Cordova when there's a deep low pressure centered in the Sound. If you were arriving from over Johnston Point with 60 or 70 knots on your tail, you were very carefully watching your DME (distance measuring equipment) and planning to lead your turn onto the final approach course. Otherwise if you waited until the needle began to move toward center or intersecting the LDA final you could slide off toward the rocks. It's about a 90 degree turn whereas you are now involved in a 60 or 70 knot crosswind approach. Moderate to severe turbulence is a common occurrence under those conditions. Add some moderate icing and lowering ceilings, guess what? You better be ready for a very spooky missed approach. Not Fun!!!

This is a safe enough procedure as long as you begin your missed at the proper missed approach point and altitude. You're still over 4,000 feet above the airport. However, there is terrain on three sides with a 3,940 foot peak very nearby.

Don't try reading the missed approach instructions for the first time at the big M, your missed approach point. You're probably going to get into trouble. For example, you're covered in ice, heavily loaded, in moderate snow with no airport in sight at the missed approach point. The missed approach instructions go something like this – "Climb via the LDA to D3.7 IVDZ, then climbing right turn to 7,000 Feet via 227 degree bearing from MNL NDB to D11.0 IVDZ then via IVDZ LDA Southwest course to JOH VOR R-319 then inbound via JOH VOR R-319 to MENTE / D20.0 JOH and hold." Try that one on when you're covered in ice, getting beaten up in moderate to severe turbulence, while all the time knowing you're over icy water and surrounded by rocks. Of course, you may not have to worry about the ice water for too long as Great Whites wander through these waters. Best to always preview these procedures before you get into the situation.

In the '80's, we didn't have the screen displays available for situational awareness. Also, you had to know what type of indicator was in your aircraft, to know whether to turn toward the needle or turn away from the needle to track the localizer back course. If you made the wrong choice, you may have only about two or three minutes to realize your mistake, correct and manage to not hit the mountain. We occasionally flew this missed approach procedure during good daylight in VFR conditions to ensure our proficiency and to observe our position relative to the terrain. Actually, it's a good idea to fly instrument approaches occasionally wherever you go, especially those in any mountainous areas.

One such missed approach occurred when an un-forecast snow storm occurred. I began taking on a ton of ice just before the missed approach point. I had a full load of anxious passengers. I could not believe this was happening as the forecast was for 5,000 foot ceilings and 10 miles visibility. At 50 feet above minimums I began powering back up. At MDA (minimum decision height) I was at full power, covered with ice, climbing at best only 500 feet per minute, in turbulence and heavy snow.

Using extreme caution, I slowly began my turn around. You betcha, I was sweating bullets - again. The engines were roaring, ice was piling up on the windshield. Glancing quickly to the side, I cycled the boots. All de-ice was working properly it seemed. I slowly began climbing out. The hazard is that anytime you get your aircraft contaminated with ice, especially the wings, your performance drops and your stall speed increases dramatically.

As the pelting ice and snow slowly diminished and things got more under control, I called back to the station. The ceiling was 1,800, visibility now 7 miles. That was good news to me. Those conditions made the VOR Approach from over the Johnston Point suitable.

That was another company specific instrument approach we were authorized to fly. That approach simply let you down over the water at a certain altitude outside the Narrows with room to turn around in case you couldn't proceed VFR. This was a valuable tool when the ceilings were below the high LDA minimums. However, this approach had one or two drawbacks. You could get three miles visibility and cancel which to me was a pretty risky option. You need to know the narrows extremely well to identify the right canyon to go into. It's easy to be a little off course and proceed up the wrong fiord. Of course they dead-end, so regardless always leave room to turn around.

What's a Fiord you ask? Well, for us airmen, they're a series of dead-end water filled canyons that open into the larger body of water. The large canyons were carved by giant glaciers that once covered the region.

About 20 minutes later, after negotiating the VOR approach, I was arriving at the Narrows at 1,500 feet. I was able to hold that altitude as I hugged the rock wall on the right. Again, I began encountering snow, visibility began to drop. Down to four or five miles now, I was straining for my visual checkpoints. I additionally had my nav set to the LDA which I began receiving. Centering up on that, I finally identified the snow covered runway and announced my intention to land. Glancing back toward the narrows I could only see whiteness. It felt good to be home. As I lined up on the runway and began easing the throttles back, I could hear several general sighs of relief from the back. As I touched down in the smooth snow covered runway a nice general round of applause broke the silence. It seemed like some of them had been through that before. As I taxied in toward the terminal, the ramp agents came jogging out toward the airplane. I had already shut down the left engine as I rolled to a stop. Stopped now, I completed my shutdown checks quickly. The ramp agent opened the door and began assisting people off the plane. Now it's my turn to let down. As I walked toward the terminal behind the last of the folks, I glanced upward, whoops, forgot for a second. Realization began to set in. I've got to either find my way through the narrow rock walled canyon or climb up through this mess if I'm going to get back to Anchorage tonight. After a short delay and a couple of coffees, the ceiling lifted just enough to meet departure minimums. I quickly got the passengers aboard. After a good briefing including the "possibility of some weather" enroute, I started the engines and began taxiing to runway 24. Pre-takeoff checks complete, I pulled out the departure plate for a quick review.

'Piece of Cake', I thought.

"Everyone ready?" I asked. I was pleasantly surprised at the visibility at this point. The snow had ended. Takeoff and climb was normal and we headed to Anchorage.

CHAPTER 27

VALDEZ - WHERE ARE WE GOING?

"I Quit!!!" was a statement I heard only one time in Alaska. If I had been in his shoes, I may have quit as well. No... probably not me.

Occasionally on this regular route to Cordova if we had no return passengers, we would layover for an hour or so, to see if help was needed for the second section to Valdez. If so, we would simply fly over empty, or "dead head" to Valdez, pick up our passengers or freight and return to Anchorage.

This particular day, I had a new co-pilot on his first flight assignment. The winds were roaring in the sound. The center of a low pressure area had drifted into the Gulf of Alaska near Seward and created gale force southeasterly winds in the area. He was already pretty shaken by the time we got to Cordova because of the turbulence, high winds and high terrain in the vicinity. On the ILS, we had very strong tail winds, had to drop like a rock to follow the glide slope, no, faster than a rock and do a circle to land in moderate to severe turbulence with poor visibility. We made it of course, I'd done it before.

The heavy snow mixed with moderate turbulence can be very disorienting when you're looking at the runway lights. A form of vertigo can occur when it seems the runway is moving around and not the aircraft. Stay on the gauges! This was one of those days when we were not getting paid enough to be there.

A missed approach in those winds could easily put you into the side of the adjacent mountain to the north. If you miss the approach, it's best to get turned around and exit the area quickly.

After a coffee and settling down for a few minutes, we checked the weather at Valdez. The ceiling was decent and the winds were generally not bad. Remember Valdez lies deep in a valley surrounded by mountains.

We took off with no problems and headed toward Johnston Point VOR to begin our instrument approach into Valdez. We departed north to intercept the Localizer at 9,000 feet. At that altitude, if you miss your turn and continue north across the localizer, you're going to hit the rocks shortly. I'd flown this route often, in good weather and bad and was carefully watching my DME (distance measuring equipment) readings, watching the mileage closely in order to safely negotiate my turn toward Valdez. Doing a double take, I was shocked to see our groundspeed. We were showing 265 knots with only 180 knots indicated! We were within three miles of the intercept point, so I began my right turn to intercept the localizer.

My co-pilot, in a nervous voice, "Where are we going?"

"I'm intercepting the localizer," I replied.

"We can't be. There's no indication!" He said loudly.

As I continued my turn, "Look at the DME. We've got 85 knots of tailwind on a 90 intercept with rocks on the other side. I'm not going to miss the intercept."

By the time I'd finished my statement and completed my turn to include an estimated drift correction, the needle came off the side and fell into place into the center of the instrument. We continued down the localizer with a 60 degree wind correction angle, practically flying sideways and were encountering moderate and occasionally severe turbulence descending over the narrows. As we dropped below the canyon walls and a few severe jolts later, the crosswinds began to let up. We finally broke out of the clouds and picked up the beautiful lights of Valdez in about our 10 o'clock position. The reason of course we were looking to our left was due to the crab angle we were holding on our final approach. The landing was normal. Paleness prevailed over on the right side of the cockpit.

We grabbed some coffee. Loaded up some freight and departed for Anchorage. On the climb out, knowing what to expect, we got lots of altitude before leaving the valley. My co-pilot was pretty quiet the rest of the trip. After we had the airplane put away and were getting ready to go home, he approached me with his paperwork and manuals, "Tony, I don't think I can do this job."

"What do you mean?" I questioned.

"I mean I don't want to do this, I quit!" as he placed his manuals on the desk.

As he started out the door, I questioned him, "Are you sure? You caught a rough evening out there and I don't blame you a bit for having second thoughts. There can be some really good days out there.

He nodded and said, "Nah. See you later."

He turned and walked out the door. I never saw him again. Actually, I really don't blame him for leaving. If that had been my first flight, I may have done the same thing. I've got to admit that, yes, this was occasionally some pretty radical flying, especially in those Piper Senecas, Cessna 402's and Beech 99's. I'm proud to say however, that in the years of flying thousands of passengers into, around and out of the sound, we never lost one. The best advice I can give you as a pilot, is to know where you are at all times. As a passenger, just know that the pilots are generally pretty sharp professionals and with the new state of the art, navigational equipment, your flight is much safer today.

"Know where you are at all times!"

CHAPTER 28

ANOTHER BAD ICE DAY!

One year in April, I was flying another second section to Valdez. That meant I was the number two aircraft on the route that morning. Wilbur's policy was to bring up whatever equipment we needed to get the job done; that is to get everyone where they needed to go in Alaska.

On this particular morning, I launched a short time after the first aircraft flown by my very good friend Captain Wayne Brockman. I'd flown with Wayne for a long time, sometimes together, but usually I was following him as he was the senior pilot and got first dibs on the scheduled runs. He was a long time Alaskan pilot and one of the best and most experienced at flying the Valdez and Cordova routes.

After takeoff from Anchorage, we were quickly in instrument conditions and began encountering moderate snow showers. Wayne and I began communicating as we proceeded up the Turnagain Arm. As we approached the Portage Pass area, Wayne in his professional captain's tone reported moderate icing. As I was five miles in trail on the same flight path, that was not good news to hear.

I was just about over the pass, when I began encountering moderate icing also. Cycling the boots about every three minutes, I increased power to maximum continuous climb power in order to hold airspeed and altitude. I was somewhat relieved to hear ATC clear Wayne to a lower altitude as he proceeded to intercept the localizer for the approach to Valdez.

Suddenly, "Hey Tony, this stuff is really getting bad! I'd call this heavy ice. We've got more terrain behind us than out here. I'm going to keep heading to Valdez."

By this time, I was also getting covered up in ice. The tip tanks had begun to grow some gnarly, antler like sculptures out the front. That must have been quite a site for the passengers as I'd never seen anything like that before or after. Rime ice was building on the leading edges of everything, including my windshield. Even with both engines at maximum power now, my airspeed slowly began to deteriorate. I began estimating the altitude of the mountain peaks below, knowing I would shortly begin trading out altitude for airspeed in order not to stall this flying chunk of ice. To get in a stall condition (meaning the wings can no longer produce enough lift to keep us flying) would mean we would shortly be looking straight down at the rocks one last time. We were beginning descent shortly into the Prince William Sound and warmer air so we both estimated we would be letting down soon and getting out of the ice.

I called on the radio, "Keep me posted Wayne, we're still over the hills, if you have to, head toward the middle of the sound." I called.

"Yeah, I already thought of that," he replied.

After three or four minutes of silence, suddenly Wayne called, "I'm descending on the localizer with full power, but getting some buffeting at 150 knots!"

"Keep your speed up Wayne; don't let that thing stall on you! Point it down, fly 160 if you have to. If you have to, leave the localizer and head out over the sound!" I answered.

"Buffeting stopped, 160 knots, 2,000 feet per minute, full power! You better get ready!" he said.

I continued behind Wayne and held 165 knots on the way down. I didn't get any buffeting, but it took full power to maintain 2,000 feet per minute descent. We both managed to meet our step down altitude minimums on the localizer and at about 4,000 feet began to shed the ice. Out of 2,000 feet most of the ice was gone and upon landing at Valdez, the airplanes were completely clear of any sign of ice.

As I taxied in I noticed Wayne's passengers were walking toward the terminal. He was unloading some cargo. I pulled up alongside and shutdown the engines. Luckily the adrenalin pump had slowed down somewhere around 4,000 feet. As I proceeded down the aisle, in my confident Captain's voice, "Welcome to beautiful Valdez, Alaska, the little Switzerland."

After the last passenger left for the terminal, I noticed Wayne checking around and under his aircraft. I drifted over and questioned, "Wayne, you alright?"

"Yeah, that was a tight one," he answered.

Looking at the planes on the ramp, he said, "Can you believe these airplanes, dry as a bone?" We both shook our heads and began walking toward the terminal, looking for that warm cup of coffee.

Charlene, our wonderful Valdez agent, pushed open the door for us and exclaimed, "What happened to you guys, you're white as ghosts!"

"Aw' Char, you wouldn't believe us if we told you. Got any of that great coffee?"

"Coming right up," she cheerfully replied.

"Wayne, what do you think about a different route home?" I asked.

"There is no different route home," he said somberly.

"Right! Two or three cups," I said, as we plopped down on a couple of overstuffed chairs in the terminal.

The double rainbow reflects an awesome feeling of protection
from above – Valdez

CHAPTER 29

MORE TROUBLE IN THE ICE

It was a cold, dark and rainy night in Cordova. I knew it was going to be a rough night as the temperature was around 32 degrees at the surface. I didn't know how rough it would become.

With one of our regular passengers in the front and eight others in the back, I departed into the night. I was heavy and climbing about 500 feet per minute. Out of about 3,000 feet, I began encountering moderate ice. 'That's okay, still climbing at a good rate', as I cycled the boots. It was pitch black now as I continued out over the icy cold sound.

As I reached 5,000 feet, I flipped on the wing ice lights. As I looked outside, I noticed my right seat passenger studying the wing on his side.

"Don't worry Ben; we should be out of this in a couple of minutes." I assured him.

As I scanned the gauges in my normal sweep, everything looked fine, except... 'This is not good.' The left oil pressure gauge was showing lower than normal oil pressure. I eased my hand onto the throttle, watching the pressure gauge as well as the temperature gauge on that engine. First was the feeling of disbelief. Then, of sincerely hoping I was looking at a gauge problem. No such luck! The pressure continued to fall rapidly now, the temperature began to climb. I flattened out of my climb and with no time to waste, I smoothly went to full power on the right engine, retarded the left engine, pulled the mixture and feathered the prop. I was now on one engine, gross weight, in moderate snow, covered with ice, over some very unforgiving terrain.

All business now, I nailed my best single engine rate of climb speed with 10 knots added for ice. I eased my flashlight onto the sick engine, to see if I could see any smoke, fire, or damage. What I saw was oozing oil coming out the back of the nacelle.

With full power on the right engine, my best rate of climb was a negative 600 feet per minute! I advised ATC and began turning back toward Cordova. Now passing through 4,000 feet, I again advised ATC of my situation and intentions.

"Cleared direct to Cordova... Keep us posted. Do you need any assistance?" ATC asked.

"You might alert the airport to have emergency crews standing by," I replied.

Now estimating I had less than five minutes remaining in the air, I didn't feel they could do a whole lot for me. I knew there was no way I could make it to the localizer for the best approach, so I opted for direct to the NDB, located just north of the field. I planned my approach much like you would in a glider I suppose.

I advised the passengers of our problem and that we would be returning to Cordova. I continually calculated time, rate of descent, speed, distance and point of landing, with ice being a major part of the equation. With the right engine churning away at full power, we were still losing 300 feet per minute as I went through 1,000 feet!

Slightly modifying my NDB-A approach and at about 500 feet, I picked up the lead in lights. Shortly, the runway came into view. On very short final, I dropped the gear and flaps and actually made a decent landing on the icy runway. I guess the situation went the best it could have.

I'd had my hands full of airplane, with no time to discuss the depth of the situation with the passengers. The only other person aware of the severity of the problem was Ben in the right seat. He held a cool head which helped to keep the passengers calm and allowed me the total focus I needed to fly the crippled, ice covered bird to the ground safely. We taxied in on one engine and parked. I breathed a sigh of relief, then told the passengers they'd have to wait for another aircraft from Anchorage to get them home.

You know what came next. I thanked God and my Guardian Angel for helping me out of what could have been a deadly situation for all of us.

A couple of hours later, another airplane and crew arrived, bearing engine parts and mechanics. I helped unload and we got the passengers headed back to town. It was the following morning when they finally got my airplane up and running. I took off with mechanics and engine parts and came on home.

No one could believe I'd saved that plane, not to mention the passengers, under those conditions. Somewhere during that very bad winter flying the sound, I picked up the handle 'Iceman'.

CHAPTER 30

TATITLEK!

Well, I believe it's one of the most attractive Native American villages I've had the privilege to serve. Located just south of the Valdez Arm and just east of Bligh Island, it's primarily inhabited by Alaskan Natives. The people are simply great folks with a long history. Their village has a natural harbor usually busy with fishing boats with one of the most prominent structures a Russian Orthodox Church.

When we weren't assigned the commuter flights, we were doing charters in various aircraft which was determined by the loads and where they were going. We flew the Seneca a lot into Tatitlek carrying groceries and other supplies. Occasionally some of the folks would fly into town to do some shopping for the day, then return in the evening.

Tatitlek, like many villages in Alaska, is isolated. The only way in or out is by boat or plane. Their runway is gravel, short and sloped, really tricky when ice is about.

One drizzly day, I flew some folks from the school board to the village. They took off with the person they were meeting and

197

I remained with the aircraft. I'd just got things buttoned up and realized it was raining more, getting really wet and getting colder. I'd just crawled back into the airplane when I noticed a man walking toward me. As he walked up, I said, "Hi, How're you doing?"

In his guttural tone, he said, "I was thinkin' you may be cold. Do you want to come up to the house and have some coffee?"

I'd not been invited to anyone's home there before. I was cold. So, I said, "Sure, I'd like to. Tony Priest's the name," as I extended my hand.

"William," as he extended his.

Other than a handshake, not much communication occurred as I followed him up the steep hill toward the village. I was glad his was one of the first homes on the road. As we entered his very rustic home I felt immediate warmth and comfort. It felt great getting out of the elements. I immediately drew near the old pot belly heater. I removed my coat and hung it on the hook by the door as he had. A single oil lantern burned on the mantle, casting soft light into the room.

"Coffee's about ready," he said.

"Sounds good," I said. "You've got a nice home here William."

The more I looked around, the more I felt memories of some of my folk's homes in Georgia in my early years. He invited me to sit down at the kitchen table. Red checkered table cloth, large heavy coffee cups, old wood burning type stove, yes, I've been here before. One of my aunts had a stove just like that. On the stove was a large iron skillet and a large blue and gray speckled metal coffee pot. As we talked, I felt more and more like I was really living a part in an olden day's saga.

He gracefully offered and poured my coffee. I continued to look around, now noticing a clothesline with clothes drying in the next room. My thoughts were again drawn to a time with no electricity, no phones.

Sitting at the table, I noticed the view was spectacular from the large window. From this hillside, you could see the harbor, the Russian Orthodox Church, my airplane by the runway, as well as a good portion of the Prince William Sound. As he reached down by his chair, "Here, try these out."

As he handed me his pair of binoculars, he began pointing out some of his favorite areas and points of interest. He said he loved to watch the large oil tankers coming out of the Valdez Arm and moving along, all weighted down with oil. He also enjoyed watching the birds, the otters and other animals and listening to the whale songs at night.

As we were finishing our coffee, suddenly his wife entered into the living room pushing a T.V. on a cart. I was somewhat surprised and stood up to introduce myself.

"This is Tony, pilot of the airplane that flew in," he said.

"I was going to watch TV," she said, giving me a quick glance and nod.

"OK, I'll go start the generator," he said as he shuffled his chair to get up.

I said, "Oh, William, I didn't know you had a TV."

He looked at me and said proudly, "Yeah, I've got a hundred channels with my new satellite dish. Come on, I'll show you."

We went out the back door and sure enough, there was his generator and huge satellite dish. Now I was shocked back into the twentieth century and somewhat amazed that this technology was in such a remote location. I didn't even think they had electricity.

The time spent with them was warm with friendship. I learned a lot about them and their way of life. They both graciously offered me to stay for dinner. However, it was getting close to takeoff time, so I thanked them greatly for their hospitality and headed down the small dirt road to the airstrip. Behind me I heard the generator fire up. I turned and waved goodbye.

As I walked down the muddy road to the airstrip, I reflected on the situation. These people are literally living two lives. This is much like a modern version of the plight of the Native Americans throughout North America. There's no wonder that drug and alcohol problems have been so prevalent within the Alaska Native population. They were and still are going through a culture shock. The Native Alaskans, recently living off the land and the sea, are suddenly plunged into the land of Hollywood.

I believe most of the Tatitlek people have handled things very well to this point, however, as in most villages, the tendency for their younger generation to be attracted to the outside world is very strong.

It wasn't long after I arrived back at the aircraft that my guys showed up.

"Ready to go?" they said cheerfully as they walked toward the airplane.

"You bet. The weather's about the same as this morning," I said as I began loading their equipment. "Did you have a good day?"

"Very good day. Thanks for bringing us out," they said as they climbed aboard.

Back to being a pilot now, I reflected briefly, 'What a wonderful moment in time.'

Little did anyone know things were about to change for the gracious people of Tatitlek. I had flown in and out of Tatitlek for some time, transporting passengers and cargo and occasionally visiting with the folks. I got to be friends with several people and the event that occurred really affected me.

The tragedy of the Exxon Valdez Oil Spill affected not only my Tatitlek friends, but the rest of the Prince William Sound. The media didn't really cover Tatitlek's plight, however this was the closest village to the accident.

I flew across the sound pretty much on a daily basis after the accident. I observed and reported the progress of the oil slick, which was creeping from island to island and steadily inching toward the village. I knew that fishing was their primary source of income and their way of life was dependent on the sea. I feared the worst was about to befall them.

As the crippled tanker Exxon Valdez continued to dump oil onto the Bligh Island shoreline, I had a bird's eye view of the oil spill from day one. The first aerial shots of the tragedy were filmed from my aircraft. Thereafter, we were busy flying news crews, oil people, clean-up people and finally supplies for the people of Tatitlek.

On one of the flights, I had a few minutes and decided to stop in and look up my friend Gary Kimkoff. After asking around, I was told he was down by the harbor. I walked down, observing the multitude of fishing boats in port.

I finally caught up with him as he stood alone, gazing at the incoming oozing black flood, just now touching the first boats.

"Hey Gary," I said as I approached.

He nodded and raised his hand and continued to gaze across the small bay.

"Gary, this doesn't look real good," I said as I viewed the sight.

As a tear welled up in Gary's eye, "Tony, you're looking at the end of our village. It's the end of our life as we know it. All the fish are dead. All the birds are dead. You can see the black oil slick moving into our harbor."

With a shaking hand, he pointed at the leading edge of what might as well have been the black plague.

The massive oil slick as it approached the
Tatitlek Village harbor.

I watched as the outer boat hulls started taking on the black, oozing oil. Glancing right and left, I saw birds, fish and small animals beginning to litter the shoreline.

What a horrible site, a horrible feeling. I can't imagine the depth of feeling of loss for those people. It must have felt like the end of the world to them. I could relate to the feeling if I imagined waking up one day, looking around my neighborhood, finding every lake and stream oozing black, sticky oil and seeing the fish, birds and animals suddenly dead and strewn all around my home. There wasn't much consoling I could offer. What can a person say? Sorry your world died?

"I'm sorry man. You've got my number. Call if we can do more or help you in any way. Call for whatever you need," I said as I shook his hand.

We headed back up toward the village. As we passed the Church, we again shook hands. I said, "Good Luck on all this." He nodded and walked away. I continued walking back toward the airstrip, speaking to a few folks along the way. As I passed William's house, I remembered some of the things we'd talked about during my visit. I looked out over the sound. There were no birds. I didn't have the heart to stop in.

On takeoff, I banked around to take another look at their harbor. It was actually sickening to watch the blackness of death devour their once vibrant and bird filled harbor.

A couple of days later and after a few phone calls, it became apparent that one of the immediate problems the folks in Tatitlek had was getting the oil out of their clothes, off their shoes, off their boats, themselves and out of just about everything in their houses.

A great friend of mine, Roland Suter, also a pilot, had some great connections with the Amway Corporation. Amway was well known throughout Alaska as having the best degreasers, as well as many other biodegradable cleaning products. After seeing the effects of their application there, I believe they are possibly the best in the entire world.

I got on the phone with Roland who picked up on the situation quickly. Roland is the kind of guy that once he embarks on a mission, there's no stopping him. He seriously got involved and dug in to get some things done. He was a personal friend of Bill Kelly, a World Wide Dream Builder Diamond in the Amway Business! Now, with Bill's lead combined with Amway's own corporate spirit and environmental concerns, within a couple of days, products and supplies began to flow in, free of charge! Amway not only sent items we had requested but began sending enough cleaning material to clean up the entire village at no charge. My comment was, "Wow, we need a bigger plane."

Joe and Anne Wilbur donated the Seneca II line aircraft for several trips. Roland and I gave our time and efforts to deliver the much needed cleaning supplies into the village. Although it seemed like a small thing at the time, I believe it helped them cope in at least one area of their lives.

Bill Kelly flew up to Anchorage from Denver at his own expense, just for this mission. It was great flying Bill and Roland to Tatitlek. The weather was reasonably good, but we had a somewhat somber flight. As we flew over the Exxon Valdez, we observed the oil slick now covering several square miles slowly invading every cove in the Prince William Sound. As we began letting down over the islands, we could see the beaches littered with black carnage, a sharp, distinct change from just a few days before. As we approached the village, we passed over the harbor, the Russian Orthodox Church and the airstrip and began circling for my landing. The entire scene seemed eerily quiet, dead.

Looking down, Bill said, "Tony, this looks real interesting, I didn't know they had a Church and all and look here, they've got a basketball court."

"Ah...Bill... That's not a basketball court. That's the runway." I replied.

It got very quiet as we turned onto our final approach. It takes intestinal fortitude just to come to Alaska the first time. To fly out to a remote seaside Native American Village takes even more courage. On April 20, 1989, Bill Kelly, who normally stood in front of 10,000 people, was standing by the eerily silent harbor in Tatitlek, Alaska, with the simple cause of helping people to help themselves.

That was Bill. Thanks Bill!

Through all our joint efforts, supplies continued to come in to Tatitlek. They were very much appreciated by everyone in the village. After Bill left, Roland and I remained active in Tatitlek for some time, assisting in any way possible. He and I later became business partners in aviation and worked together for several years. Thank you, Roland, for all you did to make things happen for the people of Tatitlek.

Since that time, things have improved slowly for the people there. But, what I hear from time to time is that the oil is still present under the rocks and in the bottom of the harbors. We all hope and pray there will never be another tragedy such as this for those people or for anyone.

On a lighter note, one evening during his stay, Bill was giving a business presentation to some folks at Roland and Jacquie's wonderful home located in a hillside community near Anchorage. As was the custom, everyone had removed their shoes, leaving them at the front door. Of course, Bill had followed suit, leaving his shoes there, also.

As he began his introduction to the group, he glanced down at his feet.

"Never shown a business plan in my socks," he stated. Then, glancing out the window, he said, "and, never saw a moose standing outside the window watching me show a business plan, or had a picture window view of the tallest mountain in America, with a live volcano erupting in the distance. You'd think I was in Alaska or something." You'd have to know Bill to understand his subtle humor. If you did know him you can hear him saying the words in your mind.

Bill Kelly, Tony Priest and Gary Komkoff in Tatitlek
Roland Suter is taking the picture.

As of this writing, Tatitlek is close to being fully recovered and is going strong. The Native American fishermen who live there are very well known for knowing the best fishing spots in the Prince William Sound. That includes some of the best Halibut fishing in Alaska. You might be lucky enough to connect with one of these guys in the future. Be sure to call before heading down there. Your only choice of travel of course is by boat or airplane. That's very typical for Alaska and generally how you find the very best Alaska has to offer. No matter how you get there, it will be an experience you will never forget.

CHAPTER 31

IN THE GAP!

Alaska flying can be hours and hours of unbelievable vistas with ever-changing scenery of majestic mountains, azure blue lakes, crystal clear rivers, oceans and pristine wilderness. You add to that every day being a different day, your feeling of adventure, meeting those daily challenges and helping others. You put forth your utmost ability. Mix all that with you as an individual, being a big part of the settlement of a new land, a new frontier. Combine all that into one feeling and you have 'ALASKA!'

Of course, that's not all you get. Those hours of wonderful Alaska flying are generally interspersed with moments, or minutes, or occasionally hours or even days of stark terror. Let's just say that this was one of those minutes.

One of the closest calls I had while flying in Alaska was during a trip to Valdez in the Portage Glacier area. I was flying alone in a Cessna 402 and had approached the infamous Portage Pass. I had planned to continue through the pass at 3,000 feet as long as the weather held.

The ceiling was ragged but holding around 4,500 feet. It was very cold. Visibility was about five miles. My normal procedure was to enter over the lake, initially bearing to the right, then begin a circling left turn to get a good view of the pass to ensure it was good enough to get through. This generally worked very well and was a good safeguard for providing an out. This particular day, I entered over Portage Lake as usual. Then began my circling left turn. Suddenly, snow began. I continued my turn toward the pass as I could see the blue water of the Prince William Sound reflecting the bright sunlight over the Whittier area. I was proceeding toward the narrowest portion of the pass when I glanced off to my left. The mountains had suddenly disappeared! I quickly looked all around, seeing nothing but white snow.

Knowing I was surrounded by steep mountains on all sides, I began to drop down to maintain visibility. The ceiling was basically free falling at this point. 'Steep mountains on all sides, the ceiling dropping like a rock, only one way out – the pass'.

Looking through the pass I still had a view of the sound; however the open area was getting smaller by the second. I began accelerating toward the deteriorating hole of light now at maximum speed. I had to make it through or I might as well be playing Russian roulette, should I lose my target.

Luckily for me, while flying alone on other occasions, I had flown through the pass at extreme low level in the past, just to see where the lowest possible escape route was. Now the ceiling was a hundred feet. I'm at redline.

"Got to run the Gap," I said aloud.

Edging off to the right against the wall of the canyon, I dropped lower, now 50 feet. I eased the nose up and over a small hill, cleared a large rock on my left and dropped down into the narrow gully. Here I am again, down and dirty, trying to stay alive. Slowing now, I precariously eased one wing up, then the other to clear another large rock out-cropping. Turning with the bend in the narrow canyon, my right wingtip barely missed another large rock. Adrenalin rushed through my body as I dropped down with the rapidly descending terrain. Suddenly, the brilliant sun, the beautiful, blue Prince William Sound and the beautiful city of Whittier, popped into full view.

I could feel the warmth of the sunlight flooding the cockpit. There was an overwhelming feeling of relief.

Portage Pass from the Whittier Side on a good day

Getting a little more composure and as my pounding heart began to slow down, I banked heavily to the left to take a look back. During my turn, I, once again, thanked the Good Lord and my Guardian Angel for delivering me from the jaws of death.

I could not believe my eyes. The entire mountain range, including the pass, was gone. The clouds were now spilling out of the pass, dropping onto the surface of the water of the sound, as if trying to catch me. I later wondered how many of the 87 crash sites within the Portage Pass area were attributed to this phenomenon. It felt good to be in the sunshine.

As always, when I found that a phenomenon such as this could occur, I raised my personal minimums. Now my personal minimums for shooting the Portage Pass in the winter are 5,000 feet altitude and 10 miles visibility. I could continue on with stories about the Prince William Sound, but hopefully you caught a glimpse of what it was like for us in the eighty's.

Oh, the Sound is still there. I'm sure the mountains, the ocean waters, the rocks and the wildlife, are all still in place. It's a magical place and in general, flying there, even with the challenges, is a wonderful place to fly an airplane. If you get a chance, don't miss seeing and experiencing the beautiful Prince William Sound.

One of the things that do change is the people. I left Wilbur's in 1990, to go to work for Rocky Mountain Helicopters. I owe thanks to my good friend, Tom Milton, who was already working for them and alerted me to the position. It was a different type of flying with a different mission – med-evacs.

Although I had flown several med-evacs for Wilbur's and other carriers, this time it was the primary mission. Rocky Mountain Helicopters had the contract with Sisters of Providence

Hospital and performed operations just about anywhere. The Flight Wing was known as Life Guard Alaska.

CHAPTER 32

ANGELS IN THE NIGHT

Oh Yes! There are Angels! Spiritual Ones? Of Course! However my reference is to the flight nurses of Life Guard Alaska. Having served directly with them for several years, I developed total respect for their profession and for the individuals in particular.

If you were born in a remote village in Alaska and had any type of medical problem, you were probably picked up and brought to Anchorage for treatment by these compassionate and skilled Angels in the Night.

Providence Hospital has one of the best baby units in the world, including a well-known "preemie" section. I've watched the nurses work with these tiny premature babies, little ones hardly as big as a human hand, often fitted with monitors and so many needles and tubes you could hardly tell it was a little person.

Even though these nurses were somewhat earthly, I saw and felt the heart of them occasionally as they fought to save a life whether it was only a few hours old or an elderly person in their last days. So, to me, the flight nurses were then and are now, real Angels.

During the late 80's and early 90's, Rocky Mountain Helicopters, based in Provo, Utah, held the contract for Lifeguard Alaska. We had several aircraft and helicopters and 15 pilots on staff. We worked hard and heavy and rescued folks from areas throughout Alaska. Our territory included all of Alaska, from the North Slope village of Barrow, to the southeast, to the very remote island of Attu, at the end of the Aleutian Chain. Practically every village in Alaska was visited by our group sometime or other. Our fleet varied from the super-fast Lear 35A, to the versatile, long range, Conquest II. One of our two helicopters was the famous Llama, which we used to rescue climbers caught in the icy grip of Mt. McKinley.

Besides years of flying to many of the bush destinations, I was quite privileged to have seen even more of Alaska by flying Air Ambulance Rescues. Flying as a Medevac pilot in Alaska, your career takes on a whole new dimension. The same goes for the flight nurses. Their job is far from normal. Out there, a hundred miles from any city, a flight nurse gets to do it all.

Ask Mae! "Stuff Happens!"

One dark, overcast Alaskan night, somewhere around 11:30 PM, my obnoxious pager went off... again causing me to levitate above my warm bed!

"Tony, we have a flight, please call dispatch.....Tony, we have a flight, please call dispatch!" the pager blared.

"Where's that stupid pager... Can't shut it off!"

Stumbling out of bed, I finally found it, shut it off and called in.

"Tony, we have a flight for you down to Dutch Harbor. We've got three critical patients. It's you and Tom. Mae and Kira are the nurses."

'Dutch! Oh man...! That place is horrible in weather.'

"Sure, Joan, I'm on my way!"

'Dutch!...Middle of the night, middle of the ocean, rock walls, high winds, low ceilings, ice, no horizon, critical fuel calculations, volcano erupting, NDB approach, squirrelly winds on a short, gravel runway and critical patients! What more could I ask for?'

'Let's see. Tom Milton, one of the best pilots at Rocky. Mae and Kira, two of the sharpest and most experienced flight nurses in Alaska, Okay, we've got an A-Team! Let's get it done!'

I scrambled around, got on my long johns, my jump suit, zipped up and pulled on my boots. I took a moment, sat down on the side of the bed for about fifteen seconds. I knew this was the best I was going to feel for the next 12 to 14 hours.

"Thank you Lord for this day which is a privilege and an opportunity for me; and thank You in advance for a successful and safe flight."

After kissing my wife goodbye, I went out the door, got into my cold car and headed for the airport. The streets were dark, cold and empty.

When I arrived at the hangar, Tom was just getting out of his car. Shortly, Mae and Kira drove up.

"Hi, Tom! Morning, Mae, Kira."

"Morning!"

"Dutch, huh?!" Tom grumbled as we exchanged glances.

"Let's check the weather. You know we can't get in there at night." I commented.

The weather was marginal, as usual, at Dutch Harbor and at Cold Bay which necessitated a very close fuel analysis. Another problem was the severe headwind forecast at the higher altitudes. Due to the winds, we elected to fly down at FL 200, or 20,000 feet however, we still had a headwind of 90 knots on the nose. On this particular night the surface winds were also a problem, blowing in excess of 50 miles per hour at both locations. The ceilings were low, ragged and constantly changing.

We decided we'd have to land at Cold Bay, wait there until closer to daylight, then head over to Dutch at daybreak. We knew it would take us more than three hours to get to Cold Bay and after discussion with Search and Rescue and the hospital, the decision was made for the ship with the accident victims, to steam north toward a rendezvous at Cold Bay.

We took off into the dark Alaskan night, knowing we were really in for it. If our timing was good however, we should get there about the same time as the ship.

The Cold Bay weather was lousy and the winds were blowing hard as usual. We executed the ILS approach, broke out of the clouds at around 400 feet and landed. And, although it was bad here, we were quite relieved by not having to fly into Dutch that day.

The Cold Bay ramp surely was a cold, dark and scary place at night. Bears randomly walked around the airport looking for a tasty meal and..., of course, we saw some signs of bears right after exiting the airplane. I hadn't planned on being dinner for any old bear and warned the nurses not to go to the terminal alone. Tom and I were busy trying to get the airplane secured and there they went, off into the night carrying nothing but a clipboard and flashlight. I remember thinking –'those nurses must be fearless knowing bears were about.'

After a few minutes, they came back and said the ship was approaching about 15 miles out and that they were going to have to go out to the ship. The Search and Rescue helicopter had made several attempts but had to turn back because of low ceilings and heavy swells. There was no other way. The ship couldn't get close enough due to the high seas.

Now, the prospects of climbing into a small boat in gale force winds gave me the woolies! Yeah, I'm a Navy man, lived on a destroyer for two years, been in a typhoon, but, from what I could see, these swells were a good 25 feet high and a 50 foot fishing boat is a lot different than a 400 foot Navy destroyer.

I was quite surprised when both nurses started gathering their gear. I must say, on that night, those nurses were showing more courage than me. I could not believe they were actually going out into that black, rolling ocean in a small boat.

To reach their patients, Mae and Kira had to climb out of the wildly pitching boat onto the ship by way of a large cargo net thrown over the side - at night! I still can't believe it, but they did it! If I had my way, I'd make sure they received a major citation or something! Perhaps by telling this story, they will be acknowledged as heroines -All in a day's work? I don't think so. They were on a selfless mission to save lives.

After a three hour standby, just about daybreak, the ambulance came driving up. We were ready to go and very happy to see these people complete with patients in tow. They looked a little ragged. Both nurses had a bad hair day look about them. Their manner was all business.

"Let's go, we've got to get out of here, we may lose one of these guys." Mae said quietly, as she began throwing her gear aboard.

We hustled to get the first one stowed, then the other and then the final one. It seemed that all three had been crushed as a result of two ships coming together in high seas. They'd either fallen overboard or were working over the side when the accident occurred. They all had IV's, tape and various bandages and looked like casualties from a war zone.

As we were about ready to get going, Mae yelled..."OK, Hold everything, we've got a problem! Get this guy off the plane; we're not getting any air in him!"

This patient weighed around 200 pounds and was the first guy we put aboard. Tom and I had a heck of a time getting him into the airplane locked down in the first place. Now, we had to quickly get undone what we'd just done. We understood the urgency of the situation however and would do whatever Mae wanted us to do.

We quickly worked our way into position to get the man from point B back to point A outside. We were used to assisting in various ways when we had to. Tom and I both had handled syringes, bagged people (with manual billows), held patients down, held patients up, helped them when they were sick, etc. This was a little different than our normal abnormalities. Mae was very serious, grabbing tools from her bag.

She yelled, "Get him around here! Get him out of the wind!"

We did and since the paramedics were also there, we got out of the way. A few minutes later, she came back around the corner, both nurses looked very ragged and now Mae was blood spattered. It seems she performed an emergency tracheotomy and got him breathing again.

I looked at Mae - what a mess, I felt like giving her a good hug. But, as we're all professionals, just doing our job, I only looked at her for a second.

Mae looked up at me, "Stuff Happens!"

"C'mon." she said, "Let's get out of here!"

Tom and I struggled to get the guy back aboard while keeping him respirated. The other two were semi-conscious and possibly aware of the critical situation. We got the door closed and began to perform our time machine magic.

As we had gotten very beat up on the way down by the heavy headwinds and turbulence, we decided to go high and take advantage of those same winds. We went to FL 330 (33,000) feet and picked up well over a hundred knots of tailwind. That Conquest II was quite a machine. It's probably my favorite aircraft in the turbo-prop class and is what I would consider a pilot's airplane.

We landed in Anchorage two hours later and were met by a couple of ambulances from Providence. We were all extremely bushed and I must say I'd gained a lot more respect for those Alaskan Flight Nurses. From what I understand, the fishermen recovered after some surgery and a good hospital stay. Guys, if you're out there, you owe a lot to those <u>Angels in the Night</u>.

Life Guard Alaska Team, 1992

Speaking of nights on the Chain, one particular night we'd landed at Cold Bay. The runway, taxiway and ramp were solidly covered by glare ice. Hey, it's my kind of runway - glare ice with a crosswind. Most of us got to be experts at landing the Conquest II in all types of conditions.

We parked the aircraft into the wind, set the parking brake and cautiously opened the door. Never mind landing on this stuff, try to stand up on it with 50 mph winds. I stepped out very carefully, but promptly found myself sliding past the tail of the plane.

That all was great fun and while I took care of the fuel, Tom and the girls, slipping and sliding, held hands as they worked their way over to the abandoned terminal to look for doughnuts or something.

Shortly after they returned, the S.A.R. Helicopter radioed in that they would be arriving in 15 minutes with our patient. We quickly wolfed down our 27 day-old honey buns from the machine, chugged down our thermos coffee and got back into the go mode.

Between the Coast Guard Team and ourselves, we finally got the patient into the aircraft. What a relief it was to be inside the Conquest with the door closed.

I again got to use some of my past ice sailing experience, as we taxied out.

"Life Guard 26PK cleared on course.
Maintain Flt Level 250."

Again, these flight nurses are not what one might consider normal nurses, if there is such a thing. A flight nurse has to know their job well beyond what would normally be considered a nurse's duties. In addition to the normally required certifications, are BLS, ACLS, TNCC, PALS, ENPC, NRP, ABLS, EMT and ATLS. Plus, add in the Alaska elements of remote villages and work sites and you kinda get the picture. They do what they have to do to save a life out there or up there.

Not only do they know their job extremely well, they also knew part of ours and had gone through some of the same survival training we had. Once a year, we combined emergency evacuation and survival training at the Anchorage Y.M.C.A. swimming pool. We had to demonstrate ditching procedures, deplaning, use of life vests, life rafts and various first aid and survival techniques in a hostile environment.

One of the drills we were tested on, was to evacuate nine people from the aircraft into the cold water, flip over an upside down life raft and get everyone into the raft, all within three and one-half minutes!

It occasionally took several tries, as about half were considered dead on the first go around. If you're still trying to flip the raft upright after five minutes or so, hypothermia has already been declared the winner.

Much to my disappointment, on my very first training event, all the girls were in jeans and sweatshirts, same as us. Don't know what I was thinking.

Ever tried to tread water in jeans? It's not easy. Flipping a ten man raft isn't easy either. Your clothes get heavy right away. The water chills you immediately. I must say I was impressed with the fight and determination those girls demonstrated. They had to be tough and physically fit. The guys, well, you know, we're all macho and all. We could tread water for two days, flip the raft 15 times in three minutes, drink swimming pool water without getting sick, all while wearing our 20 pound bunny boots.

Actually, it took a lot of team work and a coordinated effort just to get the raft upright. Getting everyone out of the water in the allotted time took a heroic effort in this realistic situation.

Other than dealing with daily emergencies, another major factor these nurses had to deal with was weather extremes. Follow us on down to Kodiak Island for a good taste of winter.

CHAPTER 33

COLD NIGHT IN KODIAK

Do you know what a minus 75 degree wind chill feels like? An Alaska flight nurse does.

We've had some very cold med-evacs. As I mentioned, my personal cut-off was minus 40 degrees ambient temperature. However, on occasion, we would get caught in more extreme conditions. Occasionally, it's not the cold, but the combination of snow, ice and wind that can really take its toll. For instance, Tom and I were flying into Kodiak late one night under very marginal conditions. Winds were extreme with ceilings coming up to minimums, then going below. It was snowing heavily on the island.

About 10 miles out, at 5,000 feet, we were instructed to enter a holding pattern. Kodiak weather had, once again, gone below landing minimums. That was something we didn't want to hear. We entered our holding pattern and shortly began to take on ice. As some of you know, that's not a very good feeling at one o'clock in the morning. We were handling the ice ok, but alerted ATC that we would need to leave this altitude as soon as possible.

After a couple of turns in holding, the reported Kodiak weather conditions returned to minimums. Anytime we had a weather situation or difficult approach to minimums, we brought the nurses into the picture. The way we looked at it, their input weighed heavily as to the extent of the emergency or decision to come back the next day. This one was an emergency that couldn't wait.

Tom and I had the numbers, trend of the weather, extent of the icing, extent of the turbulence, limitations of the aircraft and of ourselves to make the final decision.

We requested the approach and soon, we were cleared to begin our letdown into the murky, ice filled night. And, to add to the tension, we knew we were flying over an extremely turbulent ocean of black water, ice flows and rocks.

Suddenly, we began getting slammed with more severe turbulence as well as heavier icing. I placed my flashlight against the side window, covered the edge of the lens so as not to light up the cockpit.

"Ice." I mentioned. "Probably better cycle the boots again."

Tom flipped on the ice lights, "Yeah..." as he hit the switch.

As the ice blew off the wing, satisfied, he turned off the lights. We wanted it totally dark outside in order to pick up any lights from the runway environment.

Tom was captain on this trip, cool and calm and highly focused. He was doing a great job flying the aircraft by the gauges in these extreme conditions.

As we descended lower, I began standard callouts, glancing in and out of the cockpit, straining to see any sign of the runway. I glanced back at the gauges.

"Tom, 50 feet," I reported. Seconds later, "We're at minimums."

Tom began powering up. Once again, I strained to see anything. "Runway not in sight."

Tom replied, "Going missed."

We had two great nurses aboard, Kira and Janet. Both seemed cool and collected, but I'm sure they were concerned. Five hundred feet, over the water, snow, ice, turbulence and no runway, with a huge mountain in front of us. What's to worry about?

We climbed out and again elected to enter holding. This time we asked for 7,000 feet, to get up above the icing.

While in holding, we calculated we had enough fuel for about 15 minutes of holding, one more approach and if we missed again, we were headed back to Anchorage.

The weather in Anchorage was now deteriorating and we were running out of alternates.

As we briefed the nurses on our critical situation, Kira broke in, "We want that patient. He's not going to be here tomorrow. Do what you have to do!"

We continued to check the weather as we made our turns in holding.

Finally, "Kodiak automated weather – 500 feet overcast. Visibility two and one half miles, blowing snow. Winds – one five zero degrees at 33, peak gust 41 one."

Now, that might not sound that good to you, but to us, it was great.

Tom, once again, did an excellent job and 'nailed' (precisely executed) the approach. We broke out this time at 250 feet. However, we had snow on the runway and wind blowing up our tail pipes. How the next 20 seconds or so unfolded would determine both our future and the future of this mission.

Smooth, crosswind touchdown...Yes! I called the airspeeds as he eased into reverse. Things were working well. Slowing nicely now. OK Tom!

We came to a stop and Tom shut down the engines. While he finished the checklists, I unbelted and began working my way back toward the door.

Kira and Janet had pulled on their heavy jackets and were loosening the tie downs on their medical gear. I threw on my parka and gloves and cracked open the door.

"You girls ready for this?" The wind was howling around the deserted airport buildings.

Kira said, "Yeah, Let's get going."

Dressed in our parkas and snow gear, we assisted the nurses in pulling their gear out of the plane and into the waiting ambulance. The ambulance was without a patient, which was a common procedure. The first order of business was to ensure their patient was stable enough to transport, especially under these harsh conditions. This determination would be made at the hospital or clinic. Plus, they had to utilize our stretchers with airplane compatible accessories, transfer IV's, check for head injuries and other factors. For example, if the patient had a head injury, we were limited to a sea level cabin pressure. In order to do that, we would have to fly at approximately 17,000 feet.

In this case, the nurses were not sure how stable the patient was, so they couldn't give us an accurate time frame for their return. As they drove away and disappeared in the heavy snow, Tom and I exchanged glances. We ran for the door.

As we closed up the door, we were instantly relieved by the lingering warmth inside the cabin. We removed our parkas and began to relax somewhat.

However, that wonderful feeling of relief soon dissipated as we watched the heavy snow pile up on the wings. We knew we had to make a plan for being ready for an unknown wait time followed by a quick departure. It was snowing heavily and very, very cold. We knew the aircraft cabin would be below freezing shortly. With the exception of a lone fuel truck, the airport was abandoned. Reluctantly, we threw on our heavy outside gear again. We found a broom and swept the snow off, pulled on our engine covers, then again hustled inside our refuge.

After a few minutes, we realized we had to do more than keep the airplane clean. The snow had let up somewhat, however, the temperature was plummeting. We were going to be cold soaked within an hour or so. If the oil gets to a certain temperature, you cannot start a turbine aircraft. With no GPU (ground power unit) available, we knew we were in trouble. There was no question. The aircraft had to start when the nurses showed up. There was no airport equipment available and nowhere to seek shelter. Our only solution was to start the Conquest every half hour and run for 15 minutes, just to keep the oil from congealing and to keep us from freezing.

After more than three hours, we finally got the word from the nurses. The patient was stable and they were preparing to head to the airport. Getting the ambulance up to the airport in those conditions was a formidable task in itself. It was quite a relief to see the headlights coming up the otherwise deserted road. The fellow driving the ambulance did a great job.

231

We had run the airplane within the last few minutes and the cabin was still warm. We had put on some fuel and also swept the aircraft surfaces clean and were ready to go. We quickly loaded the patient and gear and closed the door. Tom jumped into the left seat while I ensured the door was locked and everyone was ready to go. By the time I got in the right seat, he had both engines running and was anxious to get out of there. Everyone on the team did their job and did it well. We were quickly airborne and into the clouds, ice, snow and turbulence. The mountains of Kodiak have claimed a lot of aircraft and a lot of lives, both military and civilian. It seemed that practically every time we were there on a Kodiak mission, it was snowing and blowing, or raining heavily with low clouds and fog blowing in and out. We've executed more than one missed approach there.

In this case, we had enough ceiling to get out. Once the aircraft's door is shut, everyone's life sits with the flight crew. If it seems to be an awesome responsibility; that's because it is.

The Conquest and Captain Tom performed flawlessly in extreme conditions. Shortly, we were looking at a beautiful night sky touting a million stars.

Life Guard Alaska Cessna 441 Conquest II
Flight Crew Office

The weather at Anchorage was tolerable, nothing like Kodiak. We had to shoot another low approach, but this time we picked up the lights early. After another beautiful Captain Tom landing and we taxied in.

As we unloaded the patient into the waiting ambulance, Janet said, "Thanks, guys. Great job!"

As they were about to shut the door on the ambulance, Kira said, "Yeah. Thanks," and then they drove away into the night.

I looked at Tom, "Dang...it's six o'clock."

"Yeah, I know," Tom replied.

We heard a heavy door slam. Our mechanic, Bob, came walking out of the hangar toward us.

"Hey, if you guys want to split, I'll take care of the airplane. You look beat."

233

"Morning, Bob. Thanks a lot," I replied.

We took him up on that, quickly filled out our paperwork and headed home. As expected, we were greeted by the headlights of rush hour traffic. Yes, this occurs even in Anchorage, Alaska.

"Wonder how it would feel to have a normal job...not!"

CHAPTER 34

SPURR - ON THE EDGE

There are some days you would like to hold on to forever.

Denali – "The Great One"

Not all Alaska flying is in bad weather. Sometimes you get those beautiful, blue sky days that you don't want to end. In

Alaska from altitude you can see forever, well, at least as far as the human eye is capable of seeing.

However, one of the most dramatic Life Guard flights for us occurred during an azure blue sky day such as the one pictured.

Captain Dave Rogers was flying left seat on this leg. I was co-captain. The nurses were Sarah and Jamie.

It began as a normal day flight to pick up a heart patient in McGrath, Alaska. We had departed Anchorage and were cleared to Flight Level 260 (26,000 feet) direct to McGrath.

The route took us directly across 11,000 foot Mt. Spurr, which was normally a point of interest for our scenic tour customers during the eighties. It was also of interest to photographers and scientists but was always billed as a dormant volcano.

However, on occasion, there were signs of geothermal activity present on the lower slopes. The State of Alaska considered at one time setting aside the south-eastern slope of the mountain for geothermal development.

We were continuing our climb out of the Cook Inlet Basin and beginning our crossing of the Alaska Range heading west passing Flight Level 200 (20,000 feet).

The sky was pure blue, not a bump anywhere. The nurses were busy studying medical charts and running checks to make sure they had things ready for the patient.

Suddenly, "Lifeguard 26PK, Anchorage Center – request," rang out.

"26PK, go ahead," I replied.

"Yeah, guys, we've had a report of seismic activity around the Mt. Spurr area. Would you take a look for us? We'd like to get a visual report."

"Sure will, 6PK." I answered.

We were both looking out the windshield ahead, but then realized we were just about over the mountain. Dave banked left and we both observed an inky black plume emitting from the top of Mt. Spurr. We were directly overhead the volcano now. The dark cloud was obscuring a portion of the top, but wasn't very high.

"Anchorage Center, 6PK," I called.

"Go ahead," ATC replied

"Yes, we're right over the mountain and there is some activity. There's a dark black ash cloud hanging just above the peak. It's not very high though. I'd estimate tops at 14,000 feet," I reported.

"Ok, thanks for your help 6PK," ATC replied. Dave rolled level and continued westbound, considering things, but not expecting anything to happen.

Three or four minutes later, a shout on the radio, "Boy! That thing just blew, it's through 450 (four five-0 – 45,000 feet) right now!!" This came from either an airline captain or military aircraft somewhere near us. The view was obviously right behind us. Quickly calculating, 'we'd been traveling at 280 KTS (320 mph) for at least three minutes,' we felt we had enough distance to make a turn to take a look. Dave began our turn to the left to get the earliest view in case we needed to make a quick exit.

As the spectacle came into view, one of the nurses, "OH, My God! What's that?"

Rising before us was something none of us had ever witnessed; something that wasn't there a couple of minutes ago -

a towering magnanimous column of smoke, ash and rocks, which seemed to hang over us.

"We've got to get out of here!" Dave said as he rolled back onto course and increased power.

Chatter began filling the airways as we quickly moved away from the explosion. The ash, dirt and rocks were falling from above us.

Dave quickly requested and was cleared to 20,000 feet in order to accelerate in our descent. After a few minutes, feeling we were clear, we turned and took a picture of the event. It looked like pictures I'd seen of a nuclear explosion!

Mt. Spurr explosive eruption.

"That was a little too close," Dave said.

"Yeah, Dave, better get the girls up here for a conference," I replied.

"Yeah," as he turned, they were already between us and anxious to discuss our situation.

We had a very critical patient waiting for us in McGrath and after some discussion, decided to continue the mission. We were only a few minutes away and our plan was to take on maximum fuel and take a look at the situation for our return. If indeed the volcano prevented us from returning to Anchorage, our alternate plan of action was to proceed to Fairbanks. Mt Spurr, or what was left of it, lay directly between us and Anchorage.

We alerted McGrath Flight Service of our quick turn status and, upon our arrival, the ambulance was standing by. We took on fuel then discussed the situation with flight service while the nurses hustled to get the patient ready

"What do you want to do Captain. It's your leg," Dave asked.

After some thought and calculations, "Dave, I think we should head toward Anchorage and attempt to get in. If the ash cloud blocks us, we'll turn and proceed to Fairbanks."

"Sounds like a good plan. I'm game," he responded.

It seemed the very large plume was tending to move northeast, verified by the winds aloft forecast. I had plenty of fuel now and good speed with the Conquest II. From the estimated plume movement reported, we felt we could beat the fallout cloud to Anchorage.

Knowing this was going to be a very intense flight, we quickly briefed everyone as to our plan and alternate plan. Everyone agreed that Fairbanks was a viable medical alternate as well as a flight plan alternate. In the worst case scenario, we would return to McGrath. We loaded the patient, got everyone aboard and departed for Anchorage.

After takeoff we turned eastbound and quickly climbed to our cruising altitude of 25,000 feet. Once on top of the cloud deck, conditions became totally clear with unlimited visibility - except for one small problem. Something larger than any super-cell I'd ever seen lay in our 12 o'clock position! It was enormous! The air was smooth and after ensuring their patient was stable, the nurses joined us in the cockpit, watching the growing, ominous phenomenon.

As we got closer, however, things became more serious and intense. The nurses elected to return to their seats and belt up. We could actually see hot smoking boulders spewing out of the vertical shaft of the eruption. We were close enough.

Mt Spurr eruption as it appeared on our return to Anchorage

Dave snapped the photo as we went around the towering inferno. We were at 25,000 feet. The right nacelle of our Conquest II - N26PK appears in the foreground above the 14,000 foot peaks of the Alaska Range. As we got closer, we could see that altering our course to the northeast, while descending, would keep us hopefully clear of the fall-out.

We began arcing around the mushroom cloud, called center and were told that the 60,000 foot mushroom cloud was now more than 100 miles in diameter. Less than a hundred miles now from Anchorage, we realized the cloud was probably descending over the city however, the ceiling and visibility were reported to be adequate for our landing.

Now with 75 miles showing on our DME (Distance Measuring Equipment), we continued around and began our descent to remain well below the mushroom cloud. As we rounded the corner, Anchorage and the entire scene of the ominous black cloud's approach to the city came into our view.

"What do you think guys?" I questioned. Jamie came up to the cockpit.

"Let's do it," Dave said.

"If you think we can make it, I'm ok with it," Sarah yelled from the back.

"The patient will be much better off at Providence," said Jamie, as she returned to her seat.

We began our descent now direct to the runway. The race was on.

Center now had a good handle on the ash cloud and gave us continuous reports as we approached. It was clear, smooth and we were hauling. I had every gauge at its limits, including the airspeed holding at redline! From the continuous reports, we knew we could arrive before the ash cloud, so we pushed on.

At 25 miles out, we picked up a good visual angle between the runway threshold and the dark, ominous, falling ash cloud. With the power greatly reduced, we were really coming down. Not only were we watching red line speeds, but now we were watching out for NTS or negative torque sensing on the engines. This means that the props are driving the engines, not the other way around. It was a balancing act for sure.

With Dave's continued vigilance we managed to keep all the numbers in check in our attempt to slow the aircraft. He called the top of every arc precisely, which meant we could change the configuration at the absolute highest speeds without shearing off some part of the aircraft. Out of 5,000 feet we had the airport in sight and requested a visual approach.

"Lifeguard 26PK, Anchorage Approach, you are cleared for the visual approach to Anchorage International. Contact tower."

"Roger. Cleared for the visual. Thanks for your help today. Going to the tower," Dave responded.

"Anchorage Tower, Lifeguard 26PK is with you 15 out, out of 5,000, visual approach, request long landing." Dave reported in.

"Roger, Lifeguard 26PK, not in sight. You are cleared to land runway six left or right. The ash cloud is estimated less than 3,000 feet over Fire Island. You're number one, recommend best speed on final. Long landing is approved," the tower answered.

"Roger. Cleared to land runway 6, 6PK," Dave replied.

"How does it look to you Dave?" I asked.

"It's about 3,000 over Fire Island. That's pretty close," he warned.

As we turned onto a three mile left base, "You've got approach flap speed!"

"Approach flaps," I called.

"There's gear speed!" he said.

"Gear down," I called.

As we turned final over Fire Island - the ash cloud was at 2,000 feet and falling fast!

"Flap Speed!" he called

"Full flaps," I answered.

"You've got it made Tone," he said.

Due to our high speed, we touched down pretty far down the runway. As the wheels touched, I eased into reverse, slowing rapidly.

"26PK requests high speed rollout to Rocky Mountain Helicopters!" Dave called.

"Roger, 6PK taxi to parking," the tower replied.

We cleared the runway and headed toward the opening hangar doors. As we pulled up to the open doors and shutdown, Bob opened the aircraft door from the outside. With extra help, the ambulance was gone, with patient, nurses and gear in a flash. Our aircraft was quickly pulled into the hangar and the large doors closed with a bang. Everyone was relieved and we were glad to be home and inside.

After a short time, one of the guys said, "Hey, Tony, Dave, take a look outside." We went to the door. It was dark! Pitch dark! Heavy ash was falling like heavy snow.

"Let' get some masks and try to get home," I said.

Then, my thoughts turned back to home and family...the kids! 'Did they get out of school'? I soon realized we had traded one emergency situation for another.

Driving was horrible. The windshield wipers had to be used even though I knew they were scratching up the glass. As it turned out, my family was fine. The kids were home and all the doors and windows had already been taped up by my wife. I did some running around for a while and managed to round up some additional masks and supplies. Eventually, things settled down and we were all eating dinner by candle light. Still, all was well. Everyone was safe for the moment and we'd had a successful day.

It turned out to be quite an event for Anchorage and quite a memorable day for the Lifeguard Alaska team and I imagine for the patient as well.

Just another day flying in Alaska?

There's more.

CHAPTER 35

"JUMP START THIS ONE!"

Barrow, Alaska, what a trip. I believe it was Tom and I arguing over a dimly lit orb in the night sky. I thought it was a moon rise. He thought it was the sun. Later, on our return, we had one orange orb on each horizon. It's not a wonder the geese fly in circles occasionally during spring and fall in Alaska.

Try this one. We took off from Anchorage at 10:00 PM in the dark. As we neared Barrow, the sun rose slightly above the horizon. It just doesn't compute. You have to just ignore all that, accept what you have before you and work with it.

This particular Med-Evac happened in the dead of winter. We were called in around 9:15 PM. Bob Pryor was my co-captain that night.

There were twin babies born in Barrow. Both were hanging on to life by a thread. Our job was to transport them from Barrow to Anchorage.

It was the middle of the night of course, in the middle of winter. The Siberian Express was roaring across northernmost Alaska. The flight nurses were Mary and Sharon.

The temperature was minus 38. Winds were blowing 30 to 40 miles per hour creating a wind chill of around minus 50 degrees. Looking at the wind direction, I realized we had close to a direct crosswind to deal with. 'Not a problem,' I thought.

We arrived without incident, unloaded the dual incubation units and watched the ambulance and nurses disappear into the night. We proceeded to prepare the aircraft for our return to Anchorage.

After about an hour, while we were standing by, the winds again began to pick up. Now they were more into the 50 to 60 mph range. Now, I'm concerned. Now, we have blowing snow perpendicular to the runway and visibility down to a mile or less. We continuously contemplated our options with the rapidly changing conditions. After an hour or so the ambulance arrived with the nurses and our miniature patients.

We were exposed to the biting, blowing snow, which was more ice than snow. We were separated from frost bite or worse, only by our winter gear. As we disconnected and pulled the incubators from the ambulance, I knew the thick glass was the only thing protecting the small, helpless infants. Inside their thick glassed units, it seemed that neither was aware of the extreme cold and weather on this horrific night. The whole team moved very quickly but struggled to get them inside the somewhat warm aircraft cabin. Actually, when we finally closed the door, it felt unbelievably warm. The nurses were working on the two babies continuously while Bob and I worked our way toward the cockpit from the crowded cabin.

Sharon yelled, "We've got a really small window here... Gotta get these babies to Anchorage!"

"Alright. We're good to go," I replied.

246

As I climbed into my seat, "Ready for a start, Bob?"

"Ready for start," he replied.

Both engines came up nicely and with all systems working, we began to taxi out into the heavy blowing snow. I was moving cautiously into the unmarked ramp in terrible, whiteout conditions.

"Go! Go! Go!" one of the nurses yelled. Of course, I ignored that as I had a specific, critical task ahead that required my total attention and focus. It's called finding a snow covered runway in whiteout conditions, without getting stuck in a snow drift.

We had proceeded about half way to the runway, when suddenly; I heard beeps, tones and scrambling around in the cabin.

"Stop! Stop! Stop!" one of the nurses yelled peering into the number two incubator.

"Oh man, we've got to jump start this one!" one of them said loudly.

After we were completely stopped, I glanced back to see both nurses with arms inside the incubator working franticly.

"Let's taxi back to the terminal. We may need some help here," Sharon said emphatically.

"You've got it. We're on our way back," I replied, as we completed our turn back toward the terminal building.

"Ok, we've got him going again!" Mary exclaimed.

We arrived back at the terminal and shut the engines down. She was on the phone with the doctor. Mary was working intently. A knock on the door came shortly. The doctor, with additional drugs and supplies, came aboard and worked along with the nurses for 30 or 40 minutes.

"He should make it now," the doctor reassured us as he opened the door.

We said our thanks to the doctor, closed the door and again taxied out into the blowing snow. Taxiing slowly in a mostly whiteout condition, we finally found the end of the runway and identified the runway lights.

When we pulled up to the end of the runway, the picture was one of eerie proportions. I had the runway lights and no runway. The runway was obscured by the blowing snow which was coming from a perpendicular direction to our takeoff path.

After completing our takeoff checks, I added onto my normal before takeoff briefing, "Bob, this is going to be an instrument takeoff for me. I'll plan for zero visibility. We have enough lights now to maintain our track; however with the changing winds along with the blowing snow, we could lose the lights. Also, vertigo is definitely a factor here."

"Yeah, I'm good to go. This is weird," Bob replied.

I set my heading bug and HSI (horizontal situation indicator) to the runway heading and rolled ahead slightly to make sure my wheels were straight down the runway. I knew that a few seconds into the takeoff roll I would be primarily focused on the instruments. Bob's job was to carefully monitor our position between the lights, call my speeds, then switch to instruments with me on rotation.

I brought up the power smoothly and insured the engines were set for identical thrust. I had no room for drift of any kind on the windblown ice. Within a few seconds, I was on the gauges, but also keeping track of the runway lights. Bob was calling speeds and drift from his perspective to ensure we remained on the center of the runway.

"Slight drift right," he said.

I eased a little more left rudder in. On heading, one degree left.

"Looks good - 90 knots – Rotate," Bob called out.

I eased the nose up into the V-bars in go-around attitude. No room for error.

Bob called, "Positive Climb Rate."

"Gear Up." I replied.

At 500 feet I began my turn around onto our departure heading and in less than five minutes, we were on top of the blowing snow storm. We were both quite surprised. Soon, we were in smooth conditions, with a million stars surrounding us.

"Bob, let's have a cup of coffee," I said.

"Sounds good, Captain Tone," he replied.

Things eventually settled down in the back. Mary and Sharon and the two babies seemed to be quite satisfied in the warmth of the quiet cabin. Bob and I talked about that departure for some time.

As always, it was good to see the lights of Anchorage again.

After a few weeks at Providence, the little ones got another flight back home with their mom and a different flight crew. I hope it was a better day. I'm sure it was.

CHAPTER 36

THE WORST - C.A.T.!

Let me tell you how bad turbulence can be in Alaska. We're talking about gut-wrenching hit your head kind of turbulence - C.A.T. (Clear Air Turbulence). This incident occurred on one of those clear, windy, yet unsuspecting days.

Captain Bob Pryor and I as co-captain were dispatched along with two flight nurses to pick up a heart patient in Homer, Alaska. The wind at Anchorage was out of the east at 17 knots. There was a forecast of severe turbulence along the route, but this is a normal occurrence in Alaska. We expected to have a rough ride anytime we travel parallel to the Chugach Mountain range with easterly winds. As severe turbulence was expected on the leeward side of the ridges, we planned to get up high quickly and to expedite through any turbulent areas. That was nothing out of the ordinary.

As we proceeded to taxi out at Anchorage International, I noticed a Boeing 747 approaching to land on Runway Six Left. The aircraft appeared to be unusually high and flying at an odd attitude for a heavy jet on landing approach.

I mentioned to Bob, "Look at that 47. He's in a slip, cross controlled approach."

"Yeah..?" After he took a glance, "Oh Yeah."

As the apparently crippled 747 drew closer, we saw two F16's, one on each wing tip of the aircraft. As we were on the parallel taxiway, we decided to slow up a bit and keep an eye on the situation. Emergency crews were showing up all over the place and the tower finally told us to hold our position. We stopped just beyond the high speed turn off for the active runway, anticipating leaving from the intersection after things settled.

As the 747 touched down, the F 16's retracted their landing gear simultaneously and began breaking off the approach. The one on the left wingtip flew right over our heads. I assumed they were helping the aircraft maintain a constant glide path to the runway.

The huge 747 continued down to the runway in, what appeared to be, a full side slip. The huge aircraft was flying cross controlled, with one wing down, the other up, with the nose pointed 35 degrees to the right, away from the centerline.

At the last moment, he straightened the aircraft a little, just before landing and touched down on one side first, then settled to the runway. He basically greased it on or made a very smooth landing. Very little smoke came from the tires. Considering what we saw next, that pilot should have gotten a medal.

We were continuing to hold just to the side of the high speed taxi-way. The 747 continued its taxi toward us with crash trucks in trail. As he came nearer, it was obvious he had decided to turn off at our intersection. The aircraft looked very unusual with pieces hanging in the wrong places. As he exited the runway, his wing tip passed very close to us. We were practically under his wing.

"Holy cow, Bob! Look at that wing!" I remarked.

The left wing was transparent from just inside the #1 engine to the fuselage. You could see right through it. The left inboard engine... was missing!

Yes... The _entire_ engine was missing, along with a major portion of the skin of the wing. There were cables, hoses and wads of wiring and other mechanical stuff hanging down. We couldn't believe what we were looking at.

Our stare was interrupted by an announcement from the tower, "Anchorage International is closed due to debris on the runway."

I looked at Bob. "We're clear of the debris field, if we takeoff from this intersection."

"Sure, give 'em a call," Bob replied.

Before I keyed the mike, "We can let that Lifeguard go," came over the radio – possibly a supervisor call.

"Lifeguard 26PK, taxi into position and hold," instructed the control tower.

"Roger, 26 PK position and hold. What happened to the 47?" I asked. There was no answer.

Bob began his taxi out onto the runway carefully looking for FOD (foreign objects or debris). We carefully rolled down the runway a short distance to be clear of any possible debris.

"Life Guard, 26PK cleared for takeoff," the tower announced.

"Roger, 26PK cleared for takeoff."

"What happened to the 747?" Again, we had no answer. We'd paused on the runway momentarily, as it was somewhat troubling to see such extreme damage on a heavy aircraft.

"Life Guard 26PK - Cleared for immediate takeoff or taxi clear of the runway," called the tower, with urgency. "Anchorage International is closed for debris cleanup."

After short discussion, we figured it must not be any of our business. We'd competed line up checks. Bob eased the power levers forward as we began our takeoff roll.

We were quickly airborne and shortly after Bob called "Gear Up," the tower once again came on the air.

<u>"Urgent Pilot Report!</u> A Boeing 747 has reported extreme turbulence over Anchorage."

Since we had Anchorage under our left wing, Bob immediately turned hard right. There was no time for discussion. We both knew it wasn't going to be pretty. I immediately spun around to the nurses who were chatting about the patient records getting prepared for picking up their heart patient.

"Hey girls. You need to buckle up tight! Make sure nothing can come loose! We may be hitting very severe turbulence."

I didn't have to say anything further. They quickly put their charts away, started pulling straps and stashing loose items.

I looked at Bob, "This could be ugly - Might leave a mark."

We had just completed our right turn heading south toward the Turnagain Arm when, just out of 900 feet - BLAM!!! Everything hit the ceiling including our heads. That's when the screaming started in the back. Then, after encountering a severe roll to the right, Bob struggled to simply keep the aircraft right side up. He'd pulled the power back to idle trying to keep the airspeed somewhat under control. He'd just gotten the right wing up and BLAM!!! Everything hit the ceiling again, except our heads. We'd both cinched ourselves down and dropped our seats. The nurses had torqued down their seatbelts as well. By this time we were both worrying about structural integrity, hoping the wings weren't going to fold on us.

Suddenly, a severe roll again to the right, then a severe pitch down... This left us hanging in our belts. We were looking vertically through the windshield at the mud flats. We were completely out of control.

We were now about 1,500 feet, looking through the windshield at the ground. Now as a pilot, you know this is not a good thing to have happen in a turbine aircraft.

After a couple of moments, Bob regained some control and pulled us out of our dive very carefully trying not to shear the wings. After that recovery, at approximately 700 feet, we were in a position to land on the crosswind runway 32.

"Bob...we better get this thing on the ground," I said, "Could be some spar damage!"

He nodded emphatically, "We're landing!"

I keyed the mike. "May Day, May Day, May Day...Anchorage Tower, Lifeguard 26 PK...We've encountered extreme turbulence, declaring an emergency, returning for a landing on runway 32."

I'm sure they knew the serious nature of the situation and I can imagine how it must have sounded to the tower, as the nurses were screaming continuously, while I was calling May Day.

Bob and I had agreed without much discussion to get the aircraft on "terra firma," as we both knew number one, we probably had structural damage and number two; it was possibly smooth in the vicinity of the airport. It would be a good decision, considering that we make it all the way to the runway.

In the surreal world of extreme turbulence, it felt and sounded like the worst roller-coaster ride you've ever been on, complete with the screaming. Bob simply continued working the aircraft back to its normal attitude and attempted to keep us right side up. We proceeded along the shore of the Turn-again Arm, over the mud-flats and headed for runway 32.

"Anchorage Tower - We are requesting landing on runway 32," I called.

"Roger. Cleared to land - runway 32. We'll have equipment standing by."

I'm sure the tower was expecting the worst considering they were getting an earful with every transmission. That's okay, they deserved an earful. I'm sure with the nurses screams in the background; they figured we were all going to die out there. However, with Captain Bob's great experience, focus and stick and rudder flying skills, we made it through the nightmare. The turbulence ended about 400 feet on short final to the runway. Finally, when the wheels touched the asphalt, the nurses quit screaming.

It's a good thing the Cessna Conquest II was built like a tank. Most ordinary airplanes might have come apart under those conditions. I've got to tell you the pilot was built like a tank. They don't come any better.

"Thanks Captain Bob!"

We were incredulous as to why the tower didn't simply tell us the Boeing 747 had lost the engine while in extreme turbulence over downtown anchorage. The engine had fallen into the parking lot of a shopping mall! Some cars were damaged, but no one was hurt. We could have done without that thrill ride, a near death experience and canceled the flight 10 minutes ago. That was a very long five or six minutes. Now, the aircraft had to be down for a week or more, undergoing a complete airframe inspection. Of course, Bob and I did get into some heated phone discussion with the folks at the control tower.

Their reasoning was something to do with a liability issue. They had no way to substantiate the 747 captain's story that extreme turbulence had ripped the number two engine off his wing. Further, there was the issue of the engine, along with many parts, falling into the shopping mall parking lot.

Their liability issues could have gotten us killed. We were glad to verify there was extreme turbulence and were happy to substantiate the 747 pilot's claim. We were not happy about their sending us up there however. We were all alive, although a little shaken and didn't press any further than that phone call. The med-evac was canceled of course. We definitely wanted the aircraft inspected before it went anywhere else.

Don't get me wrong about those flight nurses. They're tough as nails and fearless as any bush pilot in Alaska. It's just hard not to scream when you're at 1,500 feet, upside down and getting the tar kicked out of you.

So that's how rough it can get. Just stay away from the lee side (downwind) of those mountains with 80 mile per hour easterly winds. It is hard to do since Anchorage sits at the base of those mountains on the west side.

My advice to other pilots is that when coming from the east, it's best to over-fly Anchorage at high altitude, then descend well to the west and return back to Anchorage from the west. Plan ahead and think creatively. Stay away from the rotor-producing, down slope winds. If you're a local pilot and the easterly winds are really blowing, it's probably best to remain in the bunkers.

CHAPTER 37

WORLD IMPACT!

As mentioned in previous chapters, Alaska, in 1991, was geographically a very close neighbor of the Soviet Union. We listened to Russian broadcasts over our ADF radio when on trips to Nome, or anytime we were along the northwest coast of Alaska. On a good day, you could see the Russian mainland from over the Nome area.

As most know, the Berlin Wall came down in October, 1990. However, times were still very shaky throughout the next year as the U.S.S.R. went through political change. It wasn't until December 25, 1991 that President Bush, after a phone conference with Boris Yeltsin, announced the end of the Cold War. The Hammer and Sickle Flag was lowered for the last time over the Kremlin, December 31, 1991. As the following Life Guard Alaska mission occurred prior to that date, it has been seen as a very important step forward in the building of a new and better relationship between Russia and the United States.

September 23, 1991, Providence Hospital received a call from the Governor of the Magadan Region, USSR, personally asking for the med-evac of a severely burned eight-year old boy, Anton Avdeenko, from a hospital in Magadan, USSR. The boy was to be taken down to the Shriner's Hospital burn ward in Galveston, Texas. We were less than 2,000 miles away compared to about 4,000 miles the other direction to Moscow.

At first, the task seemed totally impossible due to the general logistics, time to attain approval of multiple agencies, Soviet military obstacles, not to mention, dealing with two governments still involved in a "Cold War." Thanks to efforts by Dr. Ted Mala - Institute of Circumpolar Health Studies at the University of Alaska, James Burr – president of Rocky Mountain Helicopters and Life Guard Alaska - Providence Hospital, the first ever U.S. medevac mission, deep into the Soviet Union, was launched.

It was just a few days before this event, that Dr. Mala had met at the University of Alaska with several agencies, including the head of the KGB Border staff, to discuss possible service and coordination across a generally tense border. From comments following the meeting, it seemed that operations were deemed practically impossible, with too many miles of red tape to overcome. However, in this case, the obstacles were quickly removed, possibly due to the critical nature of the young boy's condition.

A Russian navigator and interpreter, Alexander Louney, was flown into Nome to pick up the outbound flight. Immigration, Customs and the State Department moved ahead with incredible speed in this unprecedented event. Extra measures from Washington were taken, including attaining reassurance from Moscow through the Soviet Ambassador, to insure the safe passage of our aircraft through hostile territory.

Several pilots, myself included, volunteered, however the mission would require only the Lear 35. This brought in two of the best of the best Life Guard Captains, Mike Robinson and Mike Hinds. The medical team consisted of Dr. Mala and two courageous Flight Nurses, Karen Durchow and Marilyn Belanger. Our Rocky Mountain Helicopter Base Maintenance Director and Lear 35 Guru, Bob Penny, also accompanied the flight in case of any mechanical malfunction. The flight would be to a destination far away and in the middle of the night. Should anything happen to the aircraft, Bob would become a very valuable asset.

Mike Robinson didn't seem too concerned at the time. However, he did mention they would be flying along a similar ground track of Korean Air Lines 007, which, a couple of years back was shot down by a Soviet air to air missile.

After landing at their first destination, Nome, they met up with the Russian Navigator / Interpreter, Alexander. When Mike asked about their route of flight, instead of getting a detailed flight plan, he was handed a small crumpled sheet showing their route of flight. After some examination, he was glad to see, they at least had lat/longs to work with. After opening up the crumpled paper, he read -

"Nome – Abina – Volta – Provideniya – Anadyr – Chaibuka – Morova – Magadan"...

Then, "Hey, didn't that MIG that shot down Korean 007, come out of Anadyr?" As he knew that detail, he was probably more than a little concerned.

The flight out of Nome finally launched into the night. A little over three hours later, they touched down at Magadan, deep inside the Soviet Union. The medical team sped off into the night while Bob set about checking the aircraft for any problems. He also closely monitored the quality of the Russian fuel.

The pilots were taken to the Aeroflot facility to rest and plan their return flight. Mike said everyone seemed to know who they were. Some were very friendly. Some wouldn't make eye contact and remained distant.

With their critical patient aboard around 3:00 AM, the flight left Magadan, USSR bound for Anchorage.

Somewhere around 7:00 AM, the bright lights of Anchorage came into view. Can you imagine the relief they must have all felt? With priority handling by ATC, they were on the ground quickly and rolling toward the hangar.

A few minutes later, little Anton, his mom and two courageous Flight Nurses, were on their way to Providence Hospital. Of course, the pilots and the mechanic, simply set about finishing up their mission paperwork and post flight duties and went home.

After a short stay at Providence, Anton was again transported on down to Galveston, Texas, to the Shriner's Hospital, where he received the best treatment possible and fully recovered.

If you were to ask me, I'd say the flight crew -Mike Hinds and Mike Robinson, the medical team - Dr. Ted Mala, Karen Durchow, Marilyin Belanger, the mechanic – Bob Penny and the Russian Navigator – Alexander Louney, should be nationally recognized, receive awards and possibly receive medals for this unprecedented, hazardous, historical and world changing flight.

Think about it. How would you like to have flown deep into the Soviet Union during the Cold War, on a dark, wintry night, knowing you were being tracked continuously by wartime missiles? These folks did it to save some kid's life.

When I asked the guys about it, I generally got this –

Mike Robinson, "All in a day's work, Mate."

"Nah..." from all of us,

"You guys <u>are</u> special!"

CHAPTER 38

MAKING MORE NEWS

The most publicized event and med-evac we were involved in was due to an extreme skiing accident in Valdez. If you're reading this book you've seen the video I'm sure. It's played quite often on extreme sports shows.

The video is not of us but of the skier flipping end over end, down a steep, 3,000 foot snow covered, rocky, mountain slope. It's amazing that he survived. Obviously he was an extremely fit athlete.

It turned out to be one of the most difficult med-evacs we'd had. That included the paramedics and the nurses.

The patient had a serious head injury which required he be kept totally conscious the entire time. They couldn't sedate him or give him anything except localized anesthetics. He had a broken femur, head injuries and was simply in a lot of pain.

For example, we were attempting to load the 200 pound guy into the aircraft from an icy ramp. We had him on a stretcher at shoulder height, part way in the door, when the nurse at his head started yelling for a syringe. Due to the circumstance, I had to pass the syringe from one to the other, while holding up my side of the stretcher on the slippery ice. I slipped somewhat, heard my shoulder crack, but held my position. My shoulder still bothers me today. But, like many in the emergency occupational fields, we look at the small injuries as just a part of the job. The twinges I get always remind me of that moment in time.

He was complaining heavily, yelling occasionally, then proceeded to get sick, over the side of the stretcher. Luckily, the nurse got a bag for him immediately. Other than bandages, he had a steel rod extending down below his ankle, which we were told, if bumped, could make him bleed to death.

Somehow we managed to eventually get him in and secure the stretcher. We kept the cabin at sea level pressure due to his head injury. The nurses worked with him continuously and he seemed to relax somewhat enroute. Getting him off the plane was just about as tough as getting him aboard. At least the ramp wasn't covered with glare ice.

It's rare that the public catches a glance of our search and rescue teams, EMS (Emergency Medical Services) teams and especially, Air Ambulance (medevac) teams on missions. Generally, no one is running around with a camera at 40 below zero filming or shooting pictures while they're trying to save someone's life. This is true especially at night.

The best thing we can do is simply show our appreciation to anyone in the field helping others.

Great job, guys and girls! Thank you.

A Note of Appreciation:

Let's never forget the "team" aspect where the pilots and flight crews in the field are just a part of the picture. For every one of us privileged to be over Mt. McKinley at 25,000 thousand feet or to be flying through a pristine mountain pass, there stands hundreds that have and do put forth their efforts daily to make things happen.

From an aviation standpoint, in addition to our own training programs, we have intense simulator training programs, coming from companies dedicated to one thing – safety. We should all appreciate our ground and flight instructors. All have added something to our skills and experience.

Many government agencies such as the FAA and Flight Standards District Offices oversee operations to ensure safety. The NTSB investigates accidents and gives us feedback as to the cause and possible prevention, which we incorporate into our training programs. Air Traffic Controllers work daily at their intense job of getting us to our destinations safely. The Flight Service Stations have been a valuable asset throughout my flying career, especially in Alaska. Non-flying company management, dispatchers, station managers, fuelers and ramp attendants all contribute to every mission.

Our mechanics in the field, our maintenance directors, as well as aircraft manufacturers work closely to keep our aircraft in the air. I also have learned to appreciate the engineers who designed these flying machines.

From the medical aspect the Flight Nurses are the rock stars of course, but how they got there is a similar story.

The hospital medical programs, approved by folks we will probably never see or hear about, make this type of thing happen. The training the nurses have to accomplish is broad and intense. The supporting hospital staff, doctors, paramedics and other EMS personnel are all part of the team.

There is yet another aspect of the on-going EMS story. That is the sacrifice our families have to make when we're out there helping others. They have to hold their lives together while we're out there, sometimes living on the edge. They understand our mission, know the dangers and still support our cause.

I would like to say, "Thank you to those families and loved ones." If you know of someone in that position, you might do the same.

"What a blessing and privilege it was, to have served so many and to have been part of such an awesome team, Life Guard Alaska and Providence Hospital, the best of the best."

CHAPTER 39

FLYING IN THE RING OF FIRE

In the early years of flying in Alaska, we were led to believe that most of the local volcanoes were dormant. The reading materials, the general opinions and some scientific journals, pointed to dormancy in our lifetime. We were so convinced that, as requested, we would give scenic tours around the tops of all the local volcanoes in the surrounding mountains.

Just to the south however, located in the Cook Inlet south of Anchorage, 60 miles from Homer, is Mt. Augustine. This 4,000 foot island volcano is well known for its frequent activity.

One summer, while flying with Wilbur's, I was called in to fly a scientific research team down to Mt. Augustine. When I arrived at the airport, I realized that the Piper Seneca I was supposed to fly had been modified with a special door and electronic equipment. I was a little surprised, but after looking the aircraft over, it seemed there would be no problem in flying it.

There had been several eruptions during the week, which dropped ash over Kenai and Homer. The volcano was still very active; which was the reason for the flights.

The winds aloft had picked up, which created a good horizontal plume for analysis from below. Visibility was good near the top of the mountain which gave us a great opportunity for close up study.

As requested, I typically developed a wide orbit around the rim where most of the attention was on the plume. The flight below the plume was for analysis of both the ambient air and the light spectrums filtering through the plume and for various other tests.

During one of their last flights things got a little spookier when the technical crew told me they needed to get over the rim for pictures and additional tests. I had no problem getting near the rim at the top of the mountain as most of the smoke and vapors were steaming vertically for several thousand feet above. I carefully moved closer in until we were over the crumbling rim and looking down into the fiery pit. We orbited around the rim as they took photographs and continued testing.

Evidently an earthquake or seismic event shook loose a strong landslide inside the rim as large boulders suddenly began rolling toward the center. As they reached the bottom several minor explosions occurred. Smoke and steam were now heavier and it was obvious in the airplane that the sulfur vapors were getting more intense. Steam was spewing out of new spots and I decided it was time to move out. Just as I started my turn, they suggested we best vacate the area. We did back off for a few miles, paused to view the volcano for a short time. The tech crew felt they had enough samples, information and pictures and that we could head on home. We did. Everyone seemed happy with the results of the study.

I decided that I'm not interested in doing that again. I am especially not interested after seeing and experiencing the unpredictability and potential of these monster mountains! The two real bad boys are Mt. Redoubt and Mt. Spur. Both are close to Anchorage and underneath heavily traveled air routes. Both mountains prior to 1989 were known for occasionally emitting some smoke and vapor from their craters.

MT. REDOUBT ERUPTION 1989:

Mt. Redoubt 1989   Where's the top of the mountain?

The Mt. Redoubt eruption of 1989 created severe havoc for aviation. Rich Wilbur was the pilot of a metro liner with all seats filled and was transitioning across from Illiamna to Anchorage. He was within a few miles of Mt. Redoubt when it blew its top.

There was no warning from any source. The volcano was in his 12 o'clock position, right in front of him. He executed a very hard, steep turn and left the area with due haste! No damage was done, but had he been three minutes ahead of schedule, he wouldn't have told me the story.

The eruption went on for days with the dangerous ash cloud flowing with the winds aloft. We'd all been avoiding the ash cloud of course, canceling numerous flights, westbound and south, depending on the winds aloft and the pilot reports of where the cloud was and where it was forecast to be.

This particular evening, I was assigned Captain on Wilbur's Scheduled Flight to McGrath. The aircraft was a B-99 Airliner.

My First Officer and I were both surprised to have an FAA Inspector introduce himself just as we were closing the door.

We had a full aircraft and of course, the inspector got a front row seat right behind us.

The weather had deteriorated due to a front moving into the Anchorage bowl area.

I had continuously checked weather and didn't really like the trend I was seeing. I had made numerous calls to Flight Service, ATC and other agencies, trying to track the plume of the volcano. The best analysis showed that the plume could be near our route of flight, but they were having trouble tracking it due to the poor weather conditions and precipitation.

We decided to go ahead with the flight at this point however as we had a decent ceiling which would allow us to visually see the ash cloud should it drop into our flight path. We also had radar aboard which possibly would help us spot the ugly monstrous cloud.

We taxied out to runway 6-L and were number three for takeoff, when it started to rain more heavily, indicating an even more unstable condition. I became more uneasy about the situation in that with the increased precip I could not be sure where the plume was. I turned to the co-pilot, "Mike, I'm not going to takeoff."

"What are you thinking?" he asked.

"Aw, it's the ash cloud. With this much weather activity, I don't think we'll be able to get a visual on it, nor a reliable radar reading. It's just too chancy," I explained.

"Sounds great to me, but the company's gonna have a cow what with a full boat and all!" he answered.

"I don't care. I just don't feel good about it," I said as I turned to the inspector.

"Inspector Smith, I'm terminating this flight due to the weather. I think the conditions are too unstable and might prevent us from getting a visual on the ash cloud."

The FAA Inspector wrote something on his clipboard he'd been using to do his check and said, "Well, that looks like good judgment to me. Let's go home!"

He seemed quite relieved that his night was over. I know I was.

We told ground control our intention and got permission to taxi back to the gate. However, the Inspectors night was not over. As we finished unloading the aircraft, Randy, one of our linemen came running out. "Hey Tony, there's a 747 inbound with all four engines out!"

By this time, the airport was alive with emergency equipment rushing around and heading for the runway. It seems that a British Airways 747 had flown into the ash cloud, all four engines had flamed out and the pilot was returning to Anchorage dead-stick. Not only were all engines out, but his windshield was opaque. He was going to have to side-slip and look out an open side window to land should he actually make it to the airport. He was fully loaded with passengers and was dumping fuel.

As we all listened in, the crew got one engine operating as the aircraft plummeted through 19,000 feet. Then another came partially alive somewhere around 12,000. He had to be literally diving through the darkness and weather toward the airport.

As far as I know, he only had those two engines running when he intercepted the ILS. We all expected a disaster. This pilot would have to pull off a super-human feat to get a 300,000 pound 747 to and land on, that runway!

Amazingly, he appeared about three miles out, descending on final approach. With two or three engines out, night, unable to see out the front of the aircraft, looking out a side window, he side-slipped that huge aircraft to a perfect landing.

The only follow up I remember reading, was that he said his radar looked a little more intense and that it got very dark, just before he lost number one, number two, number three and number four engines simultaneously! We looked over the aircraft the next day. All four engines were completely destroyed. The leading edges of every part of the aircraft looked like it had been through a bead sanding machine. The windshield was white and opaque. Those folks were very lucky!

One of our Cessna 172's had an encounter with the same ash cloud several days later. It was a partly cloudy day. They were approaching Talkeetna, when suddenly, with no warning, it started raining a sand-like material down on them. The pilot hadn't noticed the snake-like plume drifting overhead. Luckily, they were in a position to land and they did so quickly. The pilot did an excellent job, shutting down the engine and side-slipping his aircraft, as his windshield became totally opaque in seconds. Other than replacing the windshield, the aircraft was saved.

Prior to these incidents, there were no training manuals I knew of, that included these last two situations. That's why they call Alaska the Last Great Frontier I suppose. Sometimes you have to write your own manuals as you go.

Down below Mt. Redoubt lies another smoking volcanic mountain, Mt. Illiamna. This huge mountain lies just southwest of Anchorage and basically marks the beginning of the Aleutian Mountain Range. As the range of mountains continues southwest, they become known as the Aleutian Islands or commonly called the Chain. This chain of volcanic islands divides the Bering Sea from the North Pacific Ocean and extends almost 2,000 miles from the mainland. There always seems to be at least one active volcano somewhere along the chain.

Just out from Mt. Illiamna, you can go through Lake Clark Pass to Lake Clark. This beautiful pristine lake has a couple of nice lodges and air service provided by some great folks. They've been going there a long time and know the area well.

On to the south is Lake Illiamna. This is a huge lake and a favorite fishing destination. On the south shore, where the Kvichak River pours into the lake, lies Igiugig. It's one of the best fishing spots on the lake accessible by floats or by a landing on the 3,000 foot dirt strip. Igiugig is about the strangest name I'd ever heard, even in Alaska. Few people know of this location and guided fishing trips are available. It's totally off the beaten path so to speak.

We'd had a few trips to Igiugig. However, this one occasion was very memorable. The charter was for several fishermen from the Lower Forty-Eight. The flight and landing were fairly uneventful except that the short, rough runway kept my attention.

As we rolled to a stop, I saw what looked like aliens approaching the airplane. On second glance, I realized these were the fishing guides with full mosquito gear and that since we had none, we were in for it. The guides were at the opening door and began handing out mosquito net hats. I warned the guys to quickly don their gear as they got out of the plane. I planned to stay aboard and depart quickly. Igiugig was having some kind of giant black fly or mosquito invasion. I'm not sure what they were, but they were definitely after our blood. The ravenous mosquitoes quickly began filling the aircraft as I was throwing their bags and gear off.

I had to step outside for a moment, when suddenly, one hit me on the forehead and, ouch. A stream of blood trickled down my face. I couldn't believe it! I did have my emergency mosquito nets and other gear in my survival pack, but knew I'd be roaring down the runway any minute headed home.

My poor guys were dodging, slapping and trying to get on their gear. They finally did. I wished them luck, shut the door and headed to Anchorage. I swatted mosquitoes all the way home. I get the willies just telling this story.

Speaking of fishing destinations, King Salmon, Dillingham and Kodiak Island all lie about 250 miles south and west of Anchorage. They are all great fly-in fishing destinations.

One day I was in the Ranger Station at King Salmon, chatting with a lady ranger, when a somewhat ragged looking individual walked in. He seemed kind of dazed and had been in the sun a lot. The man could barely talk. With a heavy European accent he began pointing at the maps on the table and explaining to the Ranger that he and his friend had been lost for over a week somewhere north of King Salmon and had just made it back. They'd been living off the land, battling mosquitoes, dodging bears and eating fish. She was astonished that they had survived and promptly rounded up his friend outside and helped them get to the clinic. I'd say, it's best to take a guided trip if you're going fishing in unknown wilderness.

Before we go down the Chain, I need to mention another extraordinary place called Katmai National Park. The park's northern boundary is marked by the 7,000 foot Mt. Douglas and begins 80 miles southwest of Homer. You've got to see this landscape to believe it. It's unbelievably beautiful in its own way. The park is home to the second largest and most powerful volcanic eruption in recorded history. All the land from the coast to King Salmon is included in the park, sometimes called "Land of Ten Thousand Smokes." It's less than 40 miles from King Salmon.

If you really want an adventure and a definite change of scenery, charter an airplane and head down there. There are several lodges in the area which are accessible by air.

Let's continue on down the Aleutian Chain.

CHAPTER 40

FLYING ON DOWN THE CHAIN

On down the chain you'll find several volcanic islands and many scattered villages and towns. Some have scheduled air service, such as Sand Point, Cold Bay and Dutch Harbor, but most however are charter destinations only. I feel very fortunate to have flown into these areas for many years without a mishap.

To me, the greatest hazards in flying the Aleutian Island area are the low ceilings and poor visibilities. You're at sea level with giant granite rocks jutting straight up out of the water.

Even if you think you know where things are, don't "scud" run anywhere, especially along the Aleutian Chain.

Flying low is one thing, but, low with poor visibility is another. Not a good idea to grope around, looking for a landmark to pop out at you. You might not like what you see.

When the ceiling is lower than 500 feet on the 'Chain' you need to be making other plans, however, if you are caught in the soup for any reason, best to make a 180 and if nothing in very short order, climb at your best angle on your 180 heading until positive you're clear of all obstacles, then determine the best way to deal with it.

I personally know of two pilots that unintentionally landed zero-zero in the Interior Tundra and lived to tell about it. Why? Not why did they live, we know that answer. They were just lucky. No, why would they do it in the first place?

The terrain along the Chain is a little more unforgiving. Too many pilots have lost their lives while low and in poor visibility conditions. It was a funny thing, that when I first came to Alaska and was working as a flight instructor in Anchorage, I ran into many pilots that were VFR (visual flight rules) only. I mean only! It didn't matter what the weather was like. On one biennial flight review, I proposed to the applicant the question of how to get out of an inadvertent IMC (instrument flying conditions) encounter while flying VFR. I don't remember his answer exactly, however one of his comments was that there were very few facilities in Alaska for instrument flight and I should get used to it.

After the flight, I pulled out a low level instrument chart and approach plates. He was amazed at the spider web-like network of airways, navaids and of the possibilities available for him to land safely at his destination should that occur.

Believe me, I'd much rather take my chances with possible ice for a while, than scud run at 100 feet in poor visibility. I think your chances of survival are better.

Another phenomena I've found flying on the Aleutian Chain is that upon entering an overcast layer, you can get a radical wind change. I've found this to be true also coming out of an overcast layer.

I think that many times the rapidly changing ceilings are caused by wind-shear and radical temperature changes, much like advection fog is created over land. This dangerous wind-shear effect seems to be the worst in the Dutch Harbor area, where it can be and has been a deadly force.

Dutch Harbor, or Unalaska, is located approximately 700 miles from Anchorage and lies on an island created by the 6,000 foot Makushin Volcano.

After arriving in the area, the instrument approach to Dutch Harbor, Unalaska, had to be one of the most unnerving approaches in existence. The runway is located in the Unalaska Bay on the back side of a tall, 1,600 foot mountain island. It's generally known by pilots who've flown in and out that there's been many accidents there, some fatal, including some FAA Inspectors in a light twin who hit the vertical rock wall on the NDB approach. The winds are erratic and that's about all you can count on.

An NDB is a non-directional beacon, a navigational aid, for getting below the clouds and finding the airport. On this particular approach, the NDB/DME included several DME (distance measuring equipment) fixes. You were descending over the ocean, to 2,000 feet, which you maintain, to a little over 5 miles from the facility. From there, you can descend to your minimum descent altitude of 700 feet at a point 3 miles from the facility.

You should never go past that fix without good visual conditions. To go any further can and has been deadly. The missed approach was to execute a 180 degree climbing turn, so you had to be careful of your radius of turn required to make the 180.

An example of some of the hazards that lie in wait were evident that day. We were on the final approach course of 166 degrees. The winds were in excess of 60 knots from the west. When we broke out that day, we were staring at the wall, a sheer rock face leading up to a 2,700 foot peak. Now, the wall is not directly in the flight path; it's just that with a 45 degree wind correction angle, you're looking at it in your windscreen and....when you're down lower, the winds slow down gradually, or possibly abruptly, which immediately gives you less required wind drift correction. So, un-correcting is what you have to do. To attempt to hold the same drift correction in poor visibility, while looking for the runway at Dutch, is not a good thing to do. With only 3 miles to go it's merely a couple of minutes until contact with the wall should you not realize your mistake. After our approach, we proceeded cautiously over toward town, circled around and made a landing.

Since the short runway is behind the mountain, it's partially hidden from view. You almost need to know where to look to see it. There's water at both ends of the runway and oh yeah, don't forget to key the red light out on base leg for automobile traffic crossing the runway! That's right. You have to click your mike on the frequency, which turns on the red light that will stop traffic from crossing the runway. Wild, huh! I believe the approach described has been discontinued - Probably a good idea.

Points of no return:

It seems that most of the time, you will encounter headwinds getting out there and many times there's a fuel and weather concern.

There's many destinations farther down the Chain that require constant vigilance of time, speed and distance to go to or to get back from. Poor weather at your destination or at any refueling stop can create a point of no return. Either you get to your destination or splash down. Survival rate out there is not very good. I have, along with lots of other pilots sweated bullets because of constantly changing weather with fuel stops few and far between.

"My belief is that you can't use the fuel left in the storage tank in Anchorage when you're several hundred miles away running low!"

"Flying on the Chain – 'Tanker up."

Japanese occupation and battles fought are evident on these remote islands.

When you get farther down the 1,600 mile Aleutian Chain, you are getting closer to Japan. For you history buffs, you know that Dutch Harbor was bombed heavily at the beginning of WWII. Subsequently, the Japanese began taking over the islands, first

Attu, then Kiska. The islands were eventually taken back by U.S. Forces, spearheaded by a group called Castner's Cutthroats, a Native American group of scouts and sharpshooters.

Attu, located approximately 1,700 miles from Anchorage, is the most remote island on the Chain. I took the picture above after landing on the island on a rare, decent weather day. I had wandered up on a small hill above the runway and discovered some ruins of battle. The island seemed to be a treasure-trove of WWII artifacts.

All of us at Life Guard Alaska performed med-evac flights from Atka, Adak, Shemya and the farthest pick up we had was Attu Island. We occasionally had trips out to other islands in the Bering Sea, including St. George and St. Paul. These trips pressed man and machine to the limit. As you can imagine and some know, flying to a small island, hundreds of miles off the coast, with a hundred knot headwind in bad weather, can and sometimes does give you a very interesting day.

Last but not least we don't won't to leave out the bears. Somehow Brown Bears and this chain of volcanic islands seem to go together. The biggest, meanest bruins on the earth live on Kodiak Island and throughout the Alaskan Peninsula and down the Chain.

Speaking of those bears, standby for 'Bob's Fair Chance.'

CHAPTER 41

BOB'S FAIR CHANCE!

Bob Pryor and I were on a trip to Dutch Harbor one day when he told me of being excited about his vacation coming up in a couple of weeks and that he and a friend, Frank Taylor, were going brown bear hunting down on the Chain.

I was about as happy as I could be for him in that my preferred system of bear hunting, should I be required to, would involve an F-16 with a 100 millimeter Gatling gun and a couple of missiles. In other words, I don't have any interest in standing on the same turf as a brown bear!

He said to me, "You know Tony, I've got a few bears under my belt and one thing I'd really like to do on this hunt, is give the bear a fair chance."

"Oh really?" I exclaimed.

He went on about their plans, what island they were flying to in his Super Cub, how long they planned to stay and so on. It was all very interesting.

Well, he left on vacation and I didn't hear anything from him for a couple of weeks. Then, one day, we were again, working together on another med-evac.

"How'd things go on your hunt, Bob?" I inquired.

He laughed and began to unwind the story. It seems that they'd left Anchorage as scheduled and had made it down to a location somewhere near Cold Bay. They were still flying, looking at possible landing spots and wondering where to make camp for the night, when suddenly they saw a couple of guys waving their arms at them from one of the small islands. They orbited briefly and realized the guys needed help. Bob picked a good landing spot and landed.

What they discovered was that the men were bear hunters, dropped off about a week before who were supposed to have been picked up three days ago! No one had showed up for them. They really wanted to get out and were trying to convince Bob to ferry them out. The stranded hunters suggested that he and Frank take over their camp, which could save them a lot of time. They also knew of at least three huge brown bears which they could possibly spot by hiking up on the small hill by the camp. Bob was going to ferry the guys out anyway and thought the guys were probably right. It would save them some time. Bears nearby would be good.

Bob spent the next few hours ferrying the stranded guys and their gear over to a nearby village where they could get some transportation to Anchorage. The hunters were very appreciative and wished them luck. I'm sure they went looking for the pilot in Anchorage that failed to pick them up!

After Bob had returned to their newly possessed camp, he and Frank decided to hike up on the hill and see if there were indeed any bear around. Sure enough, the guys had not lied. Grazing around in the small valley by the stream were three of the biggest brown bears they'd ever seen! Since there is a law in Alaska that you cannot fly and shoot the same day, they decided to turn in, get some sleep and be thoroughly rested for the next day. They checked and loaded their rifles and carefully laid them alongside and dosed off. Luckily, it was a totally quiet night with no visitors.

The morning was chilly. Bob sleepily crawled out of his sleeping bag, pulled on his boots and stepped out of the tent. It was quiet, a beautiful clear day. He went over to the fire, kicked some wood onto the still hot coals.

He went about getting the coffee pot ready as the flames began to catch up. Shortly, Frank drifted out and they both were looking around getting their bearings to this great hunting spot while sipping the fresh hot coffee.

Frank said, "Think those brownies are still down there?"

Bob replied, "I don't know. Let's step up the hill and take a look."

Bob with the Binoculars around his neck, started up the hill.

Frank said, "My knee's hurtin' this morning. I'll walk around the side of the hill."

Bob was on top of the hill shortly and began scanning the small valley.

"Yeah, Frank! There are no bears out there that I can see. I guess we'd better get going!" Bob said loudly

Bob heard some commotion coming from Frank's direction around the hill. At first he couldn't make it out but headed down the hill back to camp.

Suddenly, from around the hill came Frank, yelling, "BEAR!!! BEAR!!! BEAR!!!" Frank was headed for the tent and his gun!

Bob realized suddenly, he too had left his gun in the tent. Plus, it didn't look like Frank was going to make it! Bob headed to the tent, running as hard as he could go, knowing, if he didn't get to his rifle and kill the bear, Frank and he both would be killed.

They were all closing in on the tent simultaneously. Bob dove into the tent, grabbed his rifle and ran out to face the bear. By this time, the bear was 25 feet from Frank and 40 feet from Bob. Bob tripped and fell in a large hole, pulled his gun up and Wham! Wham! Dirt and rocks were flying as he hit the side of the hole he'd fallen into. The bear was 10 feet from Frank now. Bob realized what he'd done, got up on one knee - the barrel in the clear – and shot again. Wham! Wham! Wham!

Frank, with the gaping mouth of the bear at his back, dove into the tent. The huge bear went headlong into the tent behind Frank.

Bob, stunned for a moment, scrambled back toward the tent, fearing the worst, ready for anything. The bear was dead. Dead and on top of Frank!

He heard a muffled yell from below the bear.

"You okay Frank?"

"I think I'm ok. Get this thing off me!"

After some time, Bob managed to roll the bear enough to get Frank clear of the 1,000 pound mass of bear.

Bob pulled the bear's head around by the snout to look him in the eye, he said, "That's right! You're dead. I gave you a fair chance, didn't I?

Both Bob and Frank knew they'd made a critical mistake by not carrying their guns with them on their short recon. That mistake was almost their last.

"Well Bob, I'm glad you're sitting here with me today," I said.

"Me, too," he replied.

"Let's get the weather at Cold Bay. Maybe it's improving," I said.

"Cold Bay weather, 300 overcast, visibility 3 / 4 of a mile – snow – wind - 260 at 28 peak gust 48."

"Looks good," Bob said, as he handed me the approach plate for the ILS approach. ..."Yeah," I replied.

CHAPTER 42

MORE NOTABLE & INFLUENTIAL FOLKS

'The Last Frontier'... sounds ominous to some, sounds totally awesome to others. It obviously attracts us old war dogs with adrenalin addictions, adventurers, hunters, explorers and people just looking for vast and pristine wilderness. Others are simply looking for new and challenging opportunities, whether to make a fortune mining, building a wilderness lodge, or to take on the challenge of helping others.

Every summer this wild and diverse country seems to attract millions from the Lower Forty-eight and from all around the world. Many get there regretfully only to barely get a taste of what's there.

Most people who can afford the one or two weeks, have jobs, responsibilities, children in school and other important reasons for their short trip. To have a month is a real blessing; to have a summer is awesome. To be privileged to live and work there – well, it's about one of the best experiences a person like me could ever hope for.

I think just about everyone says one time or another, "I'd like to visit up there someday." But, the truth is, only one or two percent will actually do it. Out of that, maybe one or two percent stay for any period of time. It's a funny statistic, but with the Alaska population still at a little over a million, half live in the Anchorage area. That leaves only half of the 1,000,000 spread out over a tremendous expanse of territory. Now, you know one reason they still call it "The Last Frontier." The vastness of the diverse terrain, pristine wilderness, mixed with an extraordinary cross section of people, can be found nowhere else in the United States.

Alaska has not only attracted some tough as nails pilots and flight nurses, but also seismologists, volcanologists, oil industry folks, including pipeline, road builders, truckers, geologists, health organizations, naturalists, state and federal government personnel, the military, search and rescue, fishermen and others.

I'll never forget flying nine Russian Orthodox Priests around Mt. McKinley. One of them commented upon hearing my name, "There are nine of us Priests and our pilot's a Priest. This should be a blessed flight!" It was spectacular and one of the most beautiful days in Alaska, I'd ever seen.

I've also worked with and became friends with many Native Americans born in Alaska. There's a great Heritage Center in Anchorage you should visit. Here the culture and history of all the various indigenous people of this great land are explained.

Naturally, Alaska has also attracted some very famous folks, some of whom I met during my last years in Alaska. These people were, to me, some of the greatest people you'd ever want to meet. I've dedicated this chapter to acknowledge a couple of these people and later summarize some of the feelings and memories

I've come away with. The names are in alphabetical order, so as not to say one story is more important than the next.

BRUCE BABBITT – Secretary of the Interior:

August, 1993, while working with Security Aviation and for the awesome Mike O'Neil, it became my privilege and honor to be selected as the pilot for Bruce Babbitt's Northern Alaska tour. The flight was Single Pilot due to fuel load required.

Our aircraft was waxed and ready for the Secretary of Interior.

During his tour we traveled to and spent time at some very interesting places. Some I had not heard of until reviewing our itinerary. During the tour we visited fishermen, canneries, oil fields, mining operations and one LRRS on Barter Island, a very small island located off the North Coast of Alaska above Point Barrow!

I believe landing on Barter Island was much the same as landing on an aircraft carrier. I've never landed on a carrier but I've landed on Santa Catalina Island several times. I've heard there are similarities so I can imagine how it feels.

The runway, elevation 5 feet, sits on a spit of a small island surrounded by water. As you line up on final approach, you realize it's much like a water landing. Only a row of drums separate the gravel runway from the ocean swells and it appears you are landing below the water level. The ocean swells look definitely higher than the drums along the runway!

We didn't spend a whole lot of time there. Bruce met with some folks, took a tour of the facility and seemed anxious to depart.

The takeoff from Barter Island was just as interesting as the landing. As I rotated off the precarious, soft gravel runway I was immediately surrounded by ocean swells of varying heights, all in motion. I definitely remained on the gauges for a couple of minutes until the horizon settled down.

Our destination was Nome located on the northwest coast.

At Nome, we were met by a wonderful reception of mostly Native Americans, many in traditional dress.

There were speeches, dancing and singing, followed by a Native Alaskan Potlatch Dinner. Here, everyone contributes some local foods. It was great! Just remember, the blueberry cobbler you put in your mouth is not the blueberry cobbler your mother made down in Georgia. A delicacy of the north, Eskimo ice cream, is made from seal oil, blubber, blue berries and other available ingredients. The hospitality of the Nome folks was unsurpassed. They struck me as warm, generous, friendly and very family oriented. I remember the reverence before and during the prayer, as well as the humbleness, respect and graciousness Bruce demonstrated at the Pot Latch.

Hopefully no one's offended by the mentioning of different folks by their first names. It's just that the Alaska Frontier is a great equalizer of men. Many doctors don't want to be called Doctor; Pilots don't want any titles, even some military officers, wanted to be called by their first name, much like when you meet your maker I suppose. Something's very humbling about being in the Alaskan wilderness.

The next day, traveling south along the west coast, we visited the Red Dog Zinc Mine. The runway was narrow, dirt and gravel. The winds were blowing 25 knots across the runway, with turbulence coming off the trees and hills. As my wheels touched the gravel I quickly went into reverse, slowing rapidly. The plan was to stop prior to the trees at the end of the short runway, which we did of course.

What an amazing place! When you walk into the mine entrance, you realize it's virtually an underground city with everyone living inside the mine complex.

We toured the mine, living quarters and other facilities. Later, we toured areas, such as holding ponds and other environmental works where Bruce ensured that their processes were effective and that clear water was reentering the streams.

Some pictures were taken, however, I didn't receive the ones promised by the photographer, so maybe, if he reads this he'll send me one. By the way, if you promise your pilot pictures, be sure to get them to him or her. We don't forget.

The next day we crossed a major portion of Alaska and ended up in Fairbanks. After a dinner, we finally parted company. Bruce is a great guy. He's easy to talk to and has a great sense of humor.

On the way home that night I climbed up on top of the clouds, about 24,000 feet, in pilot terms Flight Level 240, not about, exactly. I was in smooth air, with a dark, star studded, beautiful night overhead. A light moon had just broken over the horizon reflecting on the tops of the 20,000 foot cloud deck.

I was enjoying the scene, when suddenly my gaze came upon a large object protruding out of the cloud ahead and slightly to my right.

It looked like...a rock!

I glanced back at my altimeter and at the co-pilot's altimeter, 'Yeah... FL 240. But it's definitely a rock, a big rock.'

Glancing at my DME and VOR bearing from Fairbanks, it appeared I was in the vicinity of Mt. McKinley. That sure brought home the realization as to the size of that mountain.

'Awesome!' 'Flight Level Two-Four-Oh', 24,000 feet - IFR – Large rock at 2 o clock! Make a note.'

JOHN DENVER – Singer, Song Writer and Environmentalist:

John and I crossed paths a few times. He generally stopped in at Anchorage when he was on his way to go fishing and seemed especially fond of the vast and pristine wilderness. I believe he wrote several songs about it but primarily, I believe Alaska provided a true get-away from things. I have always been a great fan of the man of Rocky Mountain High fame.

Later on, during the late 1990's, I lived in the Denver, Colorado area and spent a lot of time in the Rockies enjoying many of the sights and sounds that he sang about.

Other than his music he was a highly motivated environmentalist and inspired everyone around him with his ideas and charisma. Although I'd never flown with John, I'd heard from others, including his Lear pilots, who said he was a terrific pilot.

On one occasion we were helping him load up his Lear Jet to head home. He usually parked his jet on or near our ramp coming into and going out of Alaska.

John Denver's Lear Jet on the ramp in Anchorage
I appreciated his aircraft's Native American paint scheme.

I'd talked to him a little about environmental issues and told him that I really appreciated his video support for our Amway Business as well as other projects he had worked on. In some ways we held many of the same values and had similar interests.

299

John, in my opinion, was a totally wonderful person. He could have been a great comrade in just about any walk of life he chose. He could have been a bush pilot, nature enthusiast, fisherman, or a singer and songwriter. Regardless, it wouldn't matter. He'd still be great

We were talking a little about music one day, when I mentioned that I played the guitar since I was 16 and had come from a musical family. During the conversation, I mentioned a Christmas song I'd written - ("Keep Love in Christmas"). He seemed interested, so I ran home, got a copy and ran it over to him shortly before he left for the lower 48. I don't know if he ever tried it out or not. If he recorded it, I'd sure like to hear his take on it someday.

'Thanks, John, for your great work with the environment and most of all, Thank You for being who you were and all you gave of yourself.'

These two men were about the most publicly famous people that I came into contact with during my years in Alaska. Actually, hundreds of celebrities have visited the Last Frontier through the years. Several have made some awesome movies there.

My story is just a drop in the bucket, a big ole five gallon bucket. If you plan to come up some time, read some more history of Alaska before you come, especially the history of the aviation pioneers. There are hundreds of stories of everything you would expect from a very extraordinary group of people involved in the settlement of a new frontier. Better yet, read the stories and head north for a visit. Then, get out to some of the actual locations where certain events have taken place. In doing so, you will more than likely create a little history of your own and for Alaska.

Be careful, not to get too close. You just might want to stay!

"In summary, to have had such an awesome adventure, to have made so many lifetime friends and to be able to share my experience with others through the years, has been an incredible privilege."

"Thanks Jimmy. You started it... Alaska!!!!!"

"Pilots - Learn from the experience of others before you go to Alaska -- Read a lot!

Maintain Airspeed!

Leave yourself an Out!"

"Whoever you are and whatever you're doing in Alaska, always look out for your comrades and don't forget –

You are

BUILDING ON THE SHOULDERS OF GIANTS."

"Remember them. I do.

Call Sign – 'Iceman' -

Good Day."

Dear Alaska,

What an awesome privilege it was for me to fly through your beautiful mountain passes, over the vastness of your tundra and to see your pristine rivers, lakes and islands.

I've soaked into my soul the canvas of the soft pastel colors of your skies touting the complete spectrum of the colors of the rainbow.

I've sailed along past your majestic, snowcapped mountains. I've seen a thousand of your beautiful sunrises and sunsets of yellows, gold's and reds, sometimes at the hour of midnight.

I've sailed over your deep, aqua blue, sometimes emerald green waters strewn with the brilliant whiteness of the ice. Your crystal clear rivers, sometimes placid, were often raging as they weaved through your pristine wilderness.

I've seen firsthand the unstoppable forces of nature, humbling even the strongest and heartiest of souls.

I've watched as millions of sea birds all took flight at the same time, changing the colors of the landscape from green and blue to white.

I've shared with my kindred Alaskan people, sadness and loss, but also happiness and good cheer.

Thank You Alaska for sharing your Great Land, your wonderful people, your mystery and your challenge.

Thank You God, for allowing me to be there and to become an integral part of your beautiful Creation. Amen.

Tony Boyd Priest